AFTER EASTER

EASTER

BY ANNE DEVLIN

★

DRAMATISTS
PLAY SERVICE
INC.

★

AFTER EASTER was first performed by the Royal Shakespeare Company at the Other Place, Stratford, England, on May 18, 1994. It was directed by Michael Attenborough; the set design was by Francis O'Connor; the lighting design was by Robert Jones; the music was by Jennie Muskett; and the stage manager was Monica McCabe. The cast was as follows:

GRETA ....Stella Gonet
AOIFE..Ann Hasson
ROSE FLYNN..Doreen Hepburn
HELEN ....Katharine Rogers
EMER/ELISH..Janice McKenzie
MELDA/SILENT NUN ....Claire Carrie
MANUS FLYNN...William Houston
MICHAEL FLYNN ....Liam O'Callaghan
PAUL WATTERSON ....Sean O'Callaghan
CAMPBELL/COMMANDING OFFICER ....Roy Ward
FIRST SOLDIER..Jonathan Dean
SECOND SOLDIER..Darren Roberts

AFTER EASTER was first performed in Northern Ireland at The Lyric Players Theatre, Belfast, on November 3, 1994. It was directed by Bill Alexander; the set design was by Stuart Marshall; the costume design was by Anne Whittaker; and the lighting design was by Aidan Lacey. The cast was as follows:

GRETA...Jeanarme Crowley
AOIFE...Aingeal Grehan
HELEN ....Paula McFetridge
ROSE ....Trudy Kelly
EMER/ELISH ....Maggie Cronin
MELDA/SILENT NUN...Annie Farr
MANUS FLYNN..Peter O'Meara
MICHAEL FLYNN...Wesley Murphy
PAUL WATTERSON...Vincent Higgins
CAMPBELL/COMMANDING OFFICER..................Alan Craig
SOLDIER...Peter Ballanc

For my mother
Teresa Gertrude Ita Olivia

CHARACTERS

GRETA — Aoife's sister, who lives in Oxford. She is married to George, is thirty-seven, a teacher and was born in Northern Ireland. She has three children, twins aged eleven and a new baby.

AOIFE — She lives near Toombridge, the town in Ulster where she was born. She has five children, is married, and is also a teacher. She is thirty-five.

HELEN — She is a highly successful comrnercial artist, lives in London. She is Greta's and Aoife's sister. She is thirty-three.

ROSE — The mother of the girls, Rose Flynn is a draper in North Belfast, where she lives behind her shop with her husband, Michael, and her son Manus.

ELISH — A nun. She is Greta's cousin. Her mother Clare was Rose's sister. She is Prioress of her convent. She is thirty-six.

EMER — A nurse. She went to school with Aoife. She works at the Royal Victoria Hospital in Belfast. Like Greta and Helen she has moved from the country to the city.

MELDA — A dancer. A patient at the Royal Victoria Hospital. She is pregnant. She is very young.

MICHAEL — The father of the girls, married to Rose. He was a fisherman. He lives in Belfast with his wife and son.

MANUS — The brother of the girls. He is a music student who lives at home in Belfast. He is twenty-four.

CAMPBELL — A doctor, a psychiatrist at Tanglewood Hospital. Born in Edinburgh.

PAUL — Uniformed policeman at the Royal Victoria Hospital. Thirty-five.

FIRST SOLDIER — Northern English.

SECOND SOLDIER — Scottish.

COMMANDING OFFICER — Educated English accent.

AFTER EASTER

SCENE 1

The present.

Greta, an Irish woman in her late thirties, is sitting cross-legged on the floor: a spotlight is on her face as she speaks. A very loud screech of brakes is heard as a bus is forced to halt. She is not alone in the room. A man is standing by a window in the shadow.

GRETA.   I have often found when you can't do anything else you can always sit on the road. It's better than screaming. It makes everyone else scream. It makes me very quiet. My mother used to scream. She'd run upstairs after me and pull my hair. I'd sit behind the bedroom door for hours — with the bed pushed up against it. And she'd scream and scream and pound the door. But she couldn't get in. Nobody could. After a while she'd stop and go downstairs. And she'd forget about it. Then I'd put my head down and go to sleep. She'd shout, "Nobody loves you! Nobody loves you!" And I'd think it doesn't matter because I love me. I don't need anyone. And then I'd tickle myself, and that would make me smile. Until one day — there was a day we collected outside the university, it was a small march from the Students' Union. And just at the beginning as we linked up to start — I was in the front row, it was very peaceful — we linked arms and suddenly I had this rush of things, as if everything was suddenly centred in one place and it started to move, and it started to make me smile, and I kept trying not to smile; but the smile kept coming until I couldn't hold it back any longer and it grew and grew so big. And then we stepped forward and moved off.

7

I didn't go on any more marches after that. The rest of the day seemed very flat, it seemed to me — as if that was the point. And anyway lots of other things make me smile ... the sun shining through the bedroom window on my thighs. *(The lights in the room brighten. It is a hospital room somewhere in England. The man who is a doctor moves in on Greta).*

CAMPBELL.   Do you still think you're the Virgin Mary?

GRETA.   Och, I think everyone is the Virgin Mary. *(He shakes his head gravely at this.)*

CAMPBELL.   When asked why you refused to return to your house, you said, "It's a Protestant house."

GRETA.   Well it's true. It feels very Presbyterian, that house. I have tried. I stripped the door and sanded the floors and painted all the walls green and white — but I look at it and it's defeated me, I find I can't change it. It is a Protestant house.

CAMPBELL.   When asked about your relationship with your mother, you said, "Venus is my mother."

GRETA.   It's a line from a poem.

CAMPBELL.   What poem is that?

GRETA.   I haven't written it yet.

CAMPBELL.   That is the kind of response that's keeping you here, Greta!

GRETA.   Is it my fault if people are so literal?

CAMPBELL.   When the nurse brought in your baby, you said: "This is not my baby."

GRETA.   I was expressing my grief.

CAMPBELL.   I'm afraid the committee took it as evidence that you were still rejecting the child.

GRETA.   My baby was taken away from me at two-and-a-half weeks. When they brought it back later it wasn't my baby any more. I was grieving over the days I'd stopped breastfeeding him. He'd grown up and I knew I could never get that time back. They put him on powdered milk and it blew him up, he was fat. That was why I said, "This is not my baby." I'd lost that baby.

CAMPBELL.   I am trying to help you.

GRETA.   I want to go home.

CAMPBELL.   To your husband?

GRETA.   To my mother.

CAMPBELL.   I understand that you don't get on with your mother. Why?

GRETA.   Why what?

CAMPBELL.   Why do you want to go home to your mother?

GRETA.   I want to make my father jealous. I want to seduce my mother — in fact, I want to seduce you.

CAMPBELL.   *(He is about to leave the room)* Good-bye Greta.

GRETA.   I don't know which is worse — your moral good health or your hypocrisy!

CAMPBELL.   My hypocrisy?

GRETA.   Most men want to sleep with every attractive woman they meet. And that is normal. I want to sleep with most men and that is not normal. And I'm not supposed to say it. Isn't that the point? I'm not — supposed — to — use — the — words!

CAMPBELL.   Why won't you return to your husband?

GRETA.   My husband doesn't want me.

CAMPBELL.   Is that why you threw yourself in front of a bus?

GRETA.   But I didn't.

CAMPBELL.   You did, Greta. We have to agree about this piece of reality. A bus is a very substantial thing — it is not in your head, it is out there on the road. And this is your body, and it is real and substantial and if you put your body in front of a moving bus it will kill you. Now I have to find out if it was your intention or not. If it was your intention, you are staying here.

GRETA.   And if it wasn't my intention?

CAMPBELL.   You may be even more dangerous.

GRETA.   So either way, I'm staying here?

CAMPBELL.   Not necessarily.

GRETA.   Look, if I sat down on the road with twenty people I'd have been arrested. Because I sat down on the road on my own it was a suicide attempt. Confirms what I've always suspected — the difference between insanity and politics is only a matter of numbers!

CAMPBELL.   So you weren't trying to kill yourself — it was a political act? Why? What were you protesting about?

GRETA. *(Inaudibly.)* Boredom.

CAMPBELL. *(He hasn't heard properly)* I'm sorry?

GRETA. I was bored. I ran out of a room where some people were having dinner and I sat down on the road ... I may even have resented that one of the people — the woman giving the dinner party — had flown with the asparagus from Italy that morning. I may have been jealous that she was a rich art critic, that everyone at the table was a critic of one kind or another. And I had so far failed to be even a poor artist. I may even have minded that the art critic was my husband's mistress. I said something harsh and made some Englishman's wife cry.

CAMPBELL. Why do you resent being Irish so much?

GRETA. I don't resent being Irish — I only resent it being pointed out to me. I suppose I am beginning to resent being the only Irish person at every gathering.

CAMPBELL. Why don't you meet with some other Irish people.

GRETA. I don't know any, I live in Oxford ... Anyway it seems a bit vulgar, you know to go out looking for people who have the same or a similar accent. Oh I know it's something you English do all the time, but frankly that's a good reason for not doing it.

CAMPBELL. Why is this such a big thing with you people? I come from Scotland, but it's not important to me.

GRETA. *(She studies him.)* Och, you're a cod!

CAMPBELL. I understand you want a divorce.

GRETA. My husband says I talk too much.

CAMPBELL. You won't get custody of the children.

GRETA. What?

CAMPBELL. Do you think in your present circumstances that any court would let you have care of children?

GRETA. Oh God! then there isn't any point.

CAMPBELL. I am thinking of letting you out for Easter to stay with your sister.

GRETA. That's impossible! My sister lives in Toome.

CAMPBELL. Where?

GRETA. Toomebridge. Northern Ireland. I don't think she'd have me.

CAMPBELL. You have two sisters.

GRETA. Ah well, my other sister is a highly successful something or other. She's not in touch with the family — I haven't seen her for years.

CAMPBELL. Do you want out of here?

GRETA. Of course I want out of here. *(He goes to the door.)* Dr. Campbell? Wait! Please! *(He exits. Muttering.)* I never thought I was the Virgin Mary anyway. I just hope to Christ I'm not John the Baptist. *(Begins to sing.)*

My bonny lies over the ocean.

My bonny lies over the sea.

My bonny lies over the ocean.

Oh bring back my bonny to me.

(In a different voice.) Stop that singing! *(Begins again, falteringly.)*

Bring back, oh bring back,

Oh bring back my bonny to me, to me —

(Stops dead, because the door opens and a young woman comes in with an overnight bag. She closes the door, drops the bag noisily. She has one arm in a sling.)

AOIFE. At last!

GRETA. *(Getting slowly off the bed.)* Aoife?

AOIFE. Greta! *(They hug.)*

GRETA. What are you doing here?

AOIFE. Been waiting outside all morning.

GRETA. Are you over for long?

AOIFE. I'm here to take you out.

GRETA. Is Damion with you?

AOIFE. He's at home minding the children.

GRETA. I thought I was hallucinating.

AOIFE. The doctor says you can go for a week. He's nice. I'd stay if it was me.

GRETA. You always give the glad eye to anyone I like.

AOIFE. OK. He's not nice. I won't look at him. OK?

GRETA. What happened to your wrist?

AOIFE. I broke it chasing Damion with the carpet cleaner. It's your fault, really.

GRETA. How is it my fault?

AOIFE. When your flowers arrived on my birthday, they were

11

so beautiful and romantic I thought they might be from a lover — so did Damion. So I snatched the card off them and threw it in the fire. That was how the row broke out. All day I lived in hope that my admirer was going to arrive and take me away. My life's a mess, that house is a hole, I really hate it. Then Mammy rang up and said did you get Greta's flowers? I felt terrible because I never send you anything. And when she said you'd gone into hospital — I felt even worse. So you mustn't do it again, it's too expensive.

GRETA.   Mustn't do what again?

AOIFE.   Send me flowers.

GRETA.   Do you have many lovers?

AOIFE.   I have four or five phone numbers. Did I tell you I failed to seduce Roger Armstrong?

GRETA.   Who's Roger Armstrong?

AOIFE.   It was after a lecture and I knew his wife was away. We went out for a meal and I insisted on coffee at his house. So back we went. I pretended to be tired and disappeared off to his bedroom leaving the door open. I lay down on the bed and pretended to be asleep. But he never even came to see if I was all right. So after an hour of that I gave up and drove home. Damion was standing in the drive waiting. He's paranoid.

GRETA.   I'm so glad to see you, Aoife. You make me feel so normal.

AOIFE.   You are normal — it's the English who've a problem. What did you do to get in here?

GRETA.   I stopped a bus. George told the police I was suffering from postnatal depression.

AOIFE.   Is he having an affair?

GRETA.   I think so. She's an art critic. Diana.

AOIFE.   Why can't he have an affair without locking you up.

GRETA.   I think he wants the children — you know.

AOIFE.   I never did like him — I never understood how you could have married a cold English man.

GRETA.   It's not his fault!

AOIFE.   Oh please — please! Bend over backwards to be nice!

GRETA.   Auntie Clare married a man from Cornwall after her first husband who was Irish tried to strangle her. She lived with him for twenty-five years and I always remember her as the happiest woman I knew. I envied that family. They were a lot happier than our parents' marriage has ever been.

AOIFE. Aye, well, that's something else.

GRETA. Exactly.

AOIFE. Anyway, Uncle Frank was a Celt.

GRETA. I am a Catholic, a Protestant, a Hindu, a Moslem, a Jew.

AOIFE. All right. You married a rat.

GRETA. No. I don't believe that either.

AOIFE. Don't you dare be nice about him to me! He's committed you to mental hospital, he's got your children, his mistress, his career and on with his life. Meanwhile look at you, Greta! I could kill him.

GRETA. No. It's really not his fault.

AOIFE. Say what you like — but this I believe, the English and the Irish cannot love each other.

GRETA. My children are English.

AOIFE. Half English. If you came home and brought them up in Ireland you'd soon find they'd come all right.

GRETA. Don't be silly, my children have English accents. They'd be like fish out of water.

AOIFE. When was the last time you were home?

GRETA. I haven't been to Toome in twenty years.

AOIFE. No. I mean to visit Mummy and Daddy?

GRETA. Belfast? They didn't like George, so I stayed away.

AOIFE. And the children?

GRETA. Mammy's been at you!

AOIFE. You never go near them.

GRETA. They don't like George — any more than you do.

AOIFE. It's their grandchildren!

GRETA. And they're my children! I didn't see what was happening until it was too late.

AOIFE. Och I know. I just think everybody should go home.

GRETA. Aoife, you live three miles from where you were born. And you're happy to. You married the man next door.

AOIFE. I didn't. Damion's dad had the land by the estuary. I wanted to marry Roger Armstrong but *(Sighs.)* ... suppose you

13

can't have everything.

GRETA.   God — you're so greedy!

AOIFE.   Am I?

GRETA.   You were always like this — you always were the one to get everything. Everybody's love. Everybody's man. Everybody's land! Remember we used to sit on the top of the bus coming home from school and you used to pick the best houses and the best farms and say "that's mine. I saw it first." Even in I spy — it was yours!

AOIFE.   It was only words!

GRETA.   I'm not going to Ireland with you now and I'm never going back to live there.

AOIFE.   OK — I wasn't suggesting you should. Anyway Helen invited us to stay with her.

GRETA.   Oh my God! The humiliation of it. After all these years of failure who holds out her hand to me — bloody Helen.

AOIFE.   I know — Mammy always says she has cash registers for eyes. But she has a great flat — I mean she lives in a white loft with maple floors and blue drain pipes. I can't wait to get home and do our barn up! Anyway a week in London's what we both need.

GRETA.   How much does Helen know?

AOIFE.   She knows you've split up with George.

GRETA.   Jesus, great!

AOIFE.   Now come on — get your shoes on. Here, here's your coat. I'll ring for a taxi. (*Greta puts on her shoes and coat. Aoife exits. She looks around, touches the wall with the tips of her fingers.*)

GRETA.   Good-bye, room. (*Greta exits.*)

SCENE 2

Evening.

Helen's loft apartment. A window slants against the sky. Helen is standing with a drink in her hand thoughtfully poised when Aoife — who still manages to appear rooted and homely in this airy space — comes into the room. She has taken off her sling.

HELEN.   Well?

AOIFE.   Still sleeping. *(Helen hands her a drink.)* Thanks. *(She accepts the white wine.)* What are we going to do?

HELEN.   She needs to find a job.

AOIFE.   Och, don't be so practical. She needs to find herself first. My mammy's out of her mind about the whole thing.

HELEN.   My mother's been out of her mind for years.

AOIFE.   She worries about you as well.

HELEN.   Me? I'm flying really. There are three managerial positions in my company and I can have my pick.

AOIFE.   She thinks you hate her.

HELEN.   I don't. I love my family. I'm just very busy, that's all. My boss says slow down — your life will still be there tomorrow, but I'm afraid it won't.

AOIFE.   How long have you lived here?

HELEN.   About a year?

AOIFE.   And will you stay?

HELEN.   *(Nodding.)* I've plateaued.

AOIFE.   Plateaued? *(Looks around.)* Why have you got an American accent?

HELEN.   London isn't a good place to have an Irish accent right now. I find when I'm buying or selling an American accent gets me through the door. Whereas an Irish accent gets me followed round the store by a plainclothes security man. I'm not exaggerating.

AOIFE.   Wouldn't an English accent be better?

HELEN.   There are limits to betrayal — even for me.

AOIFE.   Suppose so. But all the same you should keep your own accent. *(A bloodcurdling wail is heard, drowning Aoife's last word. The sisters are rooted to the spot. Then, holding on to each other, Helen edges forward to the door; she is trailing Aoife. She throws open the door to the room Greta has been sleeping in and waits — .)*

HELEN.   Greta! Is that you? *(Greta appears with her arms raised to shield her face. Helen pulls her into the room they are in and takes her to sit down. Aoife puts her arms around Greta. Helen pours a*

15

drink into a tumbler.) Here!

GRETA. I've given up alcohol for Lent.

HELEN. It's lemonade. *(Greta drinks the brandy. Shudders.)* And brandy. *(To Aoife.)* She's somewhere else. She needs something to bring her back. *(Greta finishes the glass.)*

GRETA. I'm sorry. I'm really sorry.

HELEN. Why did you scream?

GRETA. I didn't scream.

AOIFE. You didn't?

HELEN. Then who screamed?

GRETA. I don't know, but it wasn't me.

AOIFE. Right enough, it didn't sound like you.

HELEN. What happened?

GRETA. The scream woke me — there was something standing at the foot of my bed, it screamed.

HELEN. Oh come on! It took me three years to find this place and all my life to afford it. It is not haunted. You are haunted.

AOIFE. What did you see?

GRETA. A figure. Long black hair, pale, very gaunt. Long white robes.

AOIFE. My God — a banshee!

HELEN. Oh, for heaven's sake! It was probably something she ate. Don't you go believing her. *(To Greta.)* You were dreaming and when you woke up you carried on dreaming and it made you scream.

GRETA. I didn't scream.

HELEN. It happens to me sometimes when I'm tired.

AOIFE. *(To Greta.)* I believe you.

GRETA. What surprised me was what I said to it.

AOIFE. You spoke to it?

HELEN. What did you say?

GRETA. What is it, Mother?

HELEN. There. It can't be a ghost. Mother's still alive.

GRETA. You don't think it might be a warning. That she's going to die.

HELEN. Look, why do you think it's Mother. She's hardly dark and thin.

16

AOIFE. She used to be — when she was younger.

HELEN. You're one as bad as the other.

AOIFE. You don't think it was —

HELEN. No.

GRETA. When it stopped screaming it just stood and stared at me, that's when I wasn't sure if it was a woman or a man. You don't think ... you don't think I'm going to die, do you?

AOIFE. I don't think it has anything to do with you at all. It might even belong to the room. It's probably an English ghost.

HELEN. What is it with you — does everything have to have a nationality? Even a ghost? *(To Greta.)* This place is not haunted. It was your own anger you were looking at!

AOIFE. Helen, when are you going to realize that you don't get people to accept your arguments by shouting louder than anybody else.

HELEN. True. But it's usually the argument they remember.

GRETA. She's right, though. I am angry. But the apparition wasn't so much anger — as — woe.

HELEN. Woe?

AOIFE. Did it speak to you?

GRETA. You heard it!

AOIFE. But no words?

GRETA. Just the thought.

AOIFE. What thought? *(Greta demonstrates the thought: beseeching.)*

GRETA. It felt as if the whole of Ireland was crying out to me.

AOIFE. God!

GRETA. That's what I thought, too. I thought: Christ.

HELEN. Now stop that!

AOIFE. Maybe, now don't misunderstand this, but maybe you should try and go to confession. It's maybe your guilt. I mean you married an English Protestant, and none of your children are baptized.

GRETA. He's not a Protestant, he's a Marxist. Anyway — I can't go to confession.

AOIFE. Of course you can. Even the IRA go to confession.

GRETA. I can't go to confession because I don't believe in it. I don't believe in God!

HELEN. Then why?

GRETA. That's why I am so angry about what's happening to me.

HELEN. What is happening to you?

GRETA. Devils! Angels! Voices! Pictures! I even get smells. The whole thing!

HELEN and AOIFE. What whole thing?

GRETA. At first I was afraid to go to sleep. Or turn out the light. But, now it happens when I'm awake and walking around in broad daylight. I mean — why's he picking on me? There's Aoife with her five Catholic children — and her good Catholic marriage. And Mass and Communion at least once a month. And he doesn't pick on her! Or even you, Helen — the way you live. Aoife says you're still lying down before married men. *(Helen looks at Aoife, but neither interrupts Greta.)* You'd think you might see the devil in the corner of the room from time to time out of guilt or something. But oh no — he comes tormenting me! Me, I'm not even a Christian. I don't want this — I don't want to be Irish. I'm English, French, German.

AOIFE. Oh, not German, surely. Nobody'd want to be German.

HELEN. Sounds like you'd really like New York.

AOIFE. Well, maybe that's it. He's chosen you because you are so clear.

HELEN. Clear — this is mud!

GRETA. How am I clear?

AOIFE. I mean transparent. Greta's not on anybody's side. And yet she's on everybody's side. She's so neutral — so he expresses himself through her.

HELEN. Wait a minute! Who is this guy we're all talking about?

AOIFE. All right — it.

GRETA. Yes. It — is right. But I don't want it — I don't want this!

HELEN. How long has this been going on?

GRETA. Since I came to England. About two years after I first arrived.

HELEN. But that's nearly —

GRETA. — fifteen years.

AOIFE. *(Quietly.)* And you never told anyone before tonight?

GRETA. *(Pause.)* Well I did, actually. I told George at the beginning. I shouldn't have. But I did. He told the doctors and that's why I won't get my kids back … probably. They think I think I'm the Virgin Mary — but it's more complicated than that.

HELEN. Who do you think you are?

GRETA. That's what I can't answer. You see, I only get a little bit of the picture at a time and it's up to me to interpret it. Once when I had that art teaching job near Exmoor. I hated that school. English Catholics. They used to call me the Irish Art Teacher. And the girls used to say in front of me — as if to offend me — as if I cared: Father So and So's a bog Irish priest. Oh God! I'm doing this again aren't I — I'm capturing you with my story. George says I do it all the time.

HELEN. Never mind George. What happened?

GRETA. Well, the first holiday was a mid-term break so we rented a house for a week. I wanted to do some painting. I hadn't painted since art college. I practically ran away. There was a half door to the house, and when you looked out at the rain falling in the glen, you could hear a stream nearby and the whole thing overwhelmed me with homesickness. I felt I was back in the glens of Antrim.

AOIFE. Up the airy mountain, down the rushy glen, we daren't go a-hunting —

GRETA. For fear of little men.

HELEN. Go on.

GRETA. Well, there we were with the rain and the radio — I was very agitated before I went to sleep as if I knew something was coming. Anyway, I must have fallen asleep eventually — I don't remember dreaming — but I remember thinking that it would be all right if I died in the night because no one would miss me.

AOIFE. We would miss you!

GRETA. I was as close to committing suicide as I have ever been in my life.

AOIFE. Never commit suicide. It's calling in death on the love you didn't get in life. It's a terrible thing for a woman to leave as an epitaph.

GRETA. I won't do it now because I have children. And I wasn't trying to commit suicide when I sat down in the road. But at that time in the house in the glen — two years after I came to England, I felt suicidal and that's when it happened.

HELEN. What?

GRETA. I — died. *(Unexpectedly the phone rings, four rings. The women remain waiting in stunned silence. The phone clicks to a loud answering machine message.)*

VOICE. *(Intimate male.)* Hi. It's me. I'm back. Give me a call. *(The answering machine clicks off. Helen looks distractedly towards the phone and at the same time looks at Greta; she is torn.)*

AOIFE. What makes you think you died?

GRETA. Because when I opened my eyes the room wasn't there. *(Pause.)* And when I put my hand out, I couldn't find George. I was completely alone.

HELEN. You're scaring me.

AOIFE. What was the room like?

GRETA. Roses everywhere. On the curtains, on the carpets, on the bedspreads. I chose that room because it wasn't so oppressive. There weren't roses on the walls as well. I swear to you I wasn't dreaming when I opened my eyes — I was lying out under the stars with the night wind on my face and I was so close to the heavens, as if I were lying on top of a mountain, that I could see quite clearly the star constellation. I was in such despair that I opened my mouth and let out a huge cry until my voice filled the whole sky. And I felt it leave my body and go up into the stars. I did. And I knew I had died that night.

HELEN. Why were you in despair?

AOIFE. What star constellation did you see?

GRETA. Sure how would I know? I don't get information, I just see things!

AOIFE. Describe it.

GRETA. There were seven stars — in an arrangement.

AOIFE. The Plough! You saw the symbol of the Irish Citizen Army!

HELEN. No!

AOIFE. Yes.

GRETA. I hate all that stuff. I really hate it.

HELEN. It's nothing to do with the Citizen Army. It could have been the Pleiades. The seven sisters.

GRETA. Yes. In fact I'm not sure that it wasn't the Pleiades that I saw.

AOIFE. You're Irish. Not Greek. It was the Plough you saw.

HELEN. What did you do about it?

GRETA. I gave up teaching in Exmoor. We moved to London … I got pregnant.

AOIFE. I always thought you threw yourself away.

GRETA. I had no self to throw away — I died, remember. I took some foreign language teaching and adult literacy classes. You know, immigrants and illiterate adults. Mostly Irish workers and confused Asian children. I taught them to read and write in English. I wanted to be English.

AOIFE. So you ignored the Plough.

GRETA. I ran as far away as I could get from Ireland.

HELEN. What went wrong?

GRETA. The visions got worse. I mean, they began to happen more often. And sometimes they'd have a playful quality, you know, I'd think birds were talking to me. Or I'd fancy someone and they'd turn up sitting behind me at the school sports day and grinning at me — except they're not really there, because they're famous or dead. I never minded those.

AOIFE. How do you know they weren't sitting behind you at the school sports?

GRETA. Robert Kennedy?

AOIFE. Yeah, you were hallucinating.

GRETA. That's what I think. I even saw Paul Robeson once.

HELEN. It's your desire.

GRETA. I know that.

AOIFE. He was m'daddy's big hero.

GRETA. It's when I get the big religious messages that worries me.

AOIFE. What big religious messages?

GRETA. Take the communion out of the churches and give

21

it to the people in the bus queues.

AOIFE.   Well that sounds harmless enough.

GRETA.   It sounds completely idiotic.

HELEN.   Don't do it. You don't have to do anything about this, you know.

GRETA.   What do you think I am — crazy? You think I'm going to rob churches and distribute communion wafers? Why is everybody so literal?

HELEN.   So you're not going to do anything about it?

GRETA.   Of course not. *(She suddenly clutches her stomach. Aoife and Helen don't notice this symptom.)*

AOIFE.   Do you think it happened because you came to England?

GRETA.   I do, yes. You see, I left Ireland in 1979, but I never arrived in England. I don't know where I went.

AOIFE.   But why doesn't Helen have visions? She's lived in London a lot longer than anyone.

HELEN.   I don't have visions; I have sex.

AOIFE.   But she has a husband!

HELEN.   It's not the same thing.

AOIFE.   Aye, right enough. *(Greta suddenly doubles up.)*

GRETA.   Oh God!

AOIFE.   What's wrong?

GRETA.   My pains are back. *(She is in agony, she drops to her knees on the floor. Helen moves quickly to her bag to get some pain killers. Brings it with a glass of water to Greta.)*

AOIFE.   That's brandy on an empty stomach.

GRETA.   It's not. It's because I'm telling you about it. I'm being punished. Oh please. *(She is writhing in agony on the floor. She takes the pill.)*

GRETA.   It knows I'm not going to obey it and it's hurting me.

HELEN.   Obey it?

GRETA.   Yes, the whole point is to resist.

HELEN.   Should we get a doctor?

GRETA.   No doctors !

AOIFE.   She'll be all right in a minute.

HELEN.   She's really very ill.

AOIFE.   How long before that pill takes effect? *(Helen looks at her watch.)*

HELEN.   Twenty minutes. Here. *(She takes a throw-over blanket from the chair and together they wrap the writhing body of their sister in it.)* I wish Chittra were here. She'd know what to do.

AOIFE.   Who's Chittra?

HELEN.   My neighbour. She's a GP. Terribly good. She explains everything to me. She knows all about the body, but she's in Goa for a holiday.

GRETA.   Nobody is to be told about this. You have to promise not to breathe a word about what has happened. If you do I'll deny everything. Promise me — not a word.

HELEN.   All right.

AOIFE.   I blame my daddy.

HELEN.   What's he got to do with it?

AOIFE.   He concentrated on her so much. He never talked to you or me like he talked to her. He thought I was brain-damaged at birth. He thought you were a capitalist.

GRETA.   He was right about both of you. *(She gasps in pain — calling out.)*

HELEN.   You're not pregnant, are you? They seem like contractions.

GRETA.   They are contractions — please hold on to me. *(The spasm of pain passes and leaves her gasping, but still.)* I think I know what is happening.

HELEN.   What is happening?

GRETA.   My voice has come back to me. After all these years. From the night it left me in Exmoor and I died. Tonight it came back. Oh I'm so happy. Do you know what this means?

AOIFE.   It means you're not dead any more, right?

GRETA.   It means that I'm back. It means that from now on everything I say will be true.

HELEN.   Why does this fill me with alarm?

GRETA.   Now all I have to do is wait —

AOIFE.   Wait?

GRETA.   To see what I am being prepared for.

HELEN.   Wait! Wait a minute! How do you know that this thing —

GRETA.   The voice!

23

HELEN. I don't know what it is — let's call it It. How do you know that It is good? Hmmh?

GRETA. I just know. I just know I'd like to go and see Mummy and Daddy tomorrow.

AOIFE. *(To Helen.)* Will you come?

HELEN. I don't know.

AOIFE. I'd prefer if you came with us. You could drive us.

HELEN. Yes I know, but I have things to do here.

AOIFE. Couldn't they wait — I mean you're quite a big fish in your organization —

GRETA. And I'd like to see Elish. I have to speak to Elish.

HELEN. No. Definitely not.

AOIFE. Why do you want to see Elish?

GRETA. Do you know where she is?

HELEN. I hate convents!

AOIFE. She's moved around a bit. I used to see her when she was in Donnybrook. But since she moved to Belfast I haven't kept in touch. Mammy'll have the address.

GRETA. I wish you wouldn't look as if you pitied me.

HELEN. Forgive me. I have problems of my own.

AOIFE. Who called you?

HELEN. A friend.

AOIFE. Is he important to you?

HELEN. If I went away — he would fall apart.

GRETA. Are you likely to go away?

HELEN. Yes — he lives with someone else.

GRETA. Oh, I see.

HELEN. No you don't see. Neither of you see! He says it's intellectual.

AOIFE. So you're not sleeping with him?

HELEN. I'm not sleeping with him — but I wish I were.

AOIFE. That old routine — he wants to leave your body out of it.

GRETA. He wants to fuck her brain.

AOIFE. Bastard.

GRETA. I said something else to the apparition.

HELEN. What?

GRETA. I said you mustn't harm my family.

24

AOIFE. That was a strange thing to say. Did it not reply?

GRETA. Nothing, just that terrible wail — as if the whole of Ireland were crying out to me.

HELEN. I think maybe I will take a few days out and drive you home tomorrow. *(The phone rings. Helen looks anxiously towards the phone. The phone clicks off. It rings again.)*

AOIFE. For heaven's sake answer the telephone or I will.

HELEN. I'm afraid in case it's him. *(Aoife gets up and picks up the phone.)*

AOIFE. Hello?... Damion? Right. OK. Thanks. I'll call you back. *(She puts down the phone.)* Daddy's had a heart attack. *(Helen looks at Greta.)*

HELEN. You and your bloody banshee! *(Darkness, only Greta is lit.)*

GRETA. After a while, when everything was quiet I'd pull the bed away from the door and go to sleep. And it would happen that in the middle of the night she'd come bursting in — and she'd stand there, trembling and frightened herself. And I'd have to put her back to bed. It only happened that summer when I was thirteen, and the others were away. It never happened any other year — and I never knew why ... *(Light on Aoife and Helen, who have remained.)*

AOIFE. He was a really sexy man, my daddy. All my friends at school fancied him.

HELEN. He didn't look like a fisherman. I liked him in his big boots. The waders.

AOIFE. Emer McGillicuddy used to say he looked like Ernest Hemingway.

HELEN. You wonder that he married such a thin woman. *(Pause.)*

GRETA. Except there was a book she'd been reading that summer — a cheap pornographic story of incest, the rape of a girl by her father. When Mother read this story it drove her mad. She used to run in screaming: "Where is he? Where are you hiding him?"

And when he came home, he took that book and he burnt it. So I knew from an early age that books were very powerful things. That some stories were dark stories and some stories were light stories — and you couldn't do very much about which ones got inside because mostly you wouldn't know until it was too late.

Until one day perhaps by chance someone would begin to tell you a story or you'd pick up a particular book, and the fine hair at the back of your neck would begin to stand up, and the sounds in the room would fade — and you would recognize it ... I did so want to be full of light.

SCENE 3

Dark.

The sound of nuns singing beautifully (the early morning office for the dead). Then it is broken off suddenly — and a deep sigh is heard. A sigh of great despair, as if heard in a dream, the downside of the singing voices.

Light.

A convent, entrance hall, Belfast. Two days later. Holy Thursday. A draped purple crucifix hangs over the hall.

A Young Sister is scrubbing a floor — making an arc; it makes a rhythmic sound. Then Greta walks towards her with a bundle of clothes in brown paper.

GRETA.   I've come to see my cousin — Elish O'Toole? *(The Younger Sister looks up; she is a novice with a short veil. She looks blankly.)* I'm Greta Cook — I mean Flynn. My mother sent these clothes for the orphanage. Rose. My mother's Rose Flynn ... She says my cousin is here. Sister — oh wait, you change your names — it's Bethany. Sister Bethany. *(The Young Sister gets up and takes her pail and hurries away. Three bells are sounded. Greta looks around. She waits. Suddenly, footsteps, a woman comes running — full of energy. She is wearing a tracksuit, her head is uncovered. She has a hairband on but the hair has spread like a bush, as if unused to the air and the light.)*

ELISH. Oh my goodness!... Are you Helen?

GRETA. No, I'm Greta.

ELISH. Greta?

GRETA. My mother sent these clothes for the children.

ELISH. Thank you. *(She takes the parcel.)* I'm sorry, I thought you must be Helen.

GRETA. Why?

ELISH. She sends us money.

GRETA. My sister Helen sends you money!

ELISH. Yes. So that we can give the children holidays. And I invited her to come and see us when she was next over. Only she never comes over — until now, when I believe — I'm so sorry about your father. We're praying for him. Have you seen him?

GRETA. Yes, briefly last night. I'm going back to the hospital tonight — he's on a heart machine; it makes it difficult to talk — but at least he knows we're here. I will get a chance, I know I will ... Is there somewhere we can talk for a moment or two?

ELISH. Yes, of course. Come, sit over — I'm free until evening prayers. *(They move across the still hall to a high-backed bench.)* So you live in ...?

GRETA. In Oxford. My husband teaches there.

ELISH. Aoife's the one I know best. Does she still live in Toome?

GRETA. Yes. She never moved.

ELISH. When I was at the convent in Donnybrook she used to come and see me. But that was many years ago.

GRETA. She has her hands full now.

ELISH. She's got four children, I believe.

GRETA. Five.

ELISH. And how many have you?

GRETA. I have two. Sorry — and a new baby.

ELISH. Where i : baby?

GRETA. At home with our nanny.

ELISH. And Helen has never married?

GRETA. No. I think she's very busy — still making money.

ELISH. Oh, she's a great girl. Let me see, Father O'Brien is in Oxford at present — do you know him?

GRETA. No I don't. I'm not exactly a Catholic success story. I'm in the process of being divorced.

ELISH. What happened?

GRETA. I'm sorry, but I'm not here for a consultation about my marriage. I wouldn't think that was exactly your territory, Sister Bethany.

ELISH. Then why have you come?

GRETA. I simply wished to explain the separation from my husband in case you mistook me for a good Catholic saint, which I'm not. My children are being brought up as Protestants.

ELISH. Och —

GRETA. And, I haven't been to any formal church practices — Mass or Communion — since I was at school. I came to see you as my cousin —

ELISH. I am a nun. I have no family.

GRETA. As my cousin and a nun, because you're about the only person who might be biased in the right direction.

ELISH. Well — go on.

GRETA. I need to smoke.

ELISH. Please.

GRETA. Why aren't you wearing a habit?

ELISH. We don't have to any more.

GRETA. It's funny; I expected a veil at least. And the hair is a shock. .

ELISH. I have a habit and a veil which I wear when I go out on special occasions.

GRETA. I can't say this — I'm sorry, I'm finding this very difficult. On the evening of 30 May 1982, in the village of Porlock in a house belonging to friends, I had a — *(Suddenly a Nun, wearing a habit and veil, appears with a tea trolley; it rattles as it comes towards them.)*

ELISH. Leave it, sister. Thank you. *(The Nun nods and disappears.)* Will you have some tea?

GRETA. Thank you. She's only brought one cup.

ELISH. The tea is for you. *(Greta receives the cup.)* Some rules never change. We don't take tea with visitors.

GRETA.   I remember ... of course, it wasn't the evening — it was morning — about 5 A.M. A flame appeared in the curtain facing my bed. It was growing bright — I was not sleeping or dreaming. I wanted to switch on the light beside me, and not taking my eye off the flame I reached out for the light switch but I could not find it. So I looked away for a second to find the switch, and when I looked back, the flame had disappeared. I remember feeling disappointed. Then I put on the light.

ELISH.   Why disappointed?

GRETA.   Because I knew that if I had lain perfectly still and simply watched the flame it would have remained and I might have learnt something. As it was I panicked and reached out to find the light. I lay for several hours with the light on just gazing at the place where the flame had been then I got up around seven and opened the curtains. I went down to the kitchen and made a cup of tea. I needed to hear some human voices. It was too early to call anybody on the telephone. So I turned on the radio — there was singing, and then a man's voice said: "Let us pray on this Pentecost Sunday ..." I am not a religious person. My father is an atheist and my husband is a Marxist. And I had ceased to be a Catholic so long ago that I had no idea when Pentecost was — I still don't.

ELISH.   It's the seventh Sunday after Easter. Which is a movable feast. You should remember that much.

GRETA.   But I'm not a believer. And yet that flame — hung there at the foot of my bed in a strange room. At lunchtime I called my husband, he came to collect me. I never spent another night in that house. I don't know why this is happening to me or what I'm supposed to do about it.

ELISH.   Where was the house?

GRETA.   I told you — in the country. Porlock.

ELISH.   I take it that this is not an isolated incident.

GRETA.   It's not an isolated incident.

ELISH.   Why were you alone at that time?

GRETA.   I was unhappy. My husband didn't want children and I did. It was the third strange experience of my life. *(Elish en-*

courages her to continue.) The second had occurred earlier in the year; on 2 February.

ELISH.   The purification.

GRETA.   We had some people in to dinner and I was relighting the candles on the table, which had burnt down and gone out. As I moved the candle to the fireplace and reached into the fire and then transferred the lit candles to the stand — the flame leapt. It lit up my hair, which at the time was long and I suddenly found myself surrounded by a curtain of flame.

ELISH.   Who put the flames out?

GRETA.   What — oh, my husband.

ELISH.   How?

GRETA.   He took my hair in his hands and beat it. *(She claps.)* Like that. A strange cry came out of my mouth — when the fire caught — it was almost as startling as the fire itself.

ELISH.   What did it sound like?

GRETA.   *(Chants.)* Ah ah ah ah ah ah. *(She makes a beautiful sound, echoing the nuns singing at the beginning.)*

ELISH.   And there was another incident? You said there were three.

GRETA.   Yes, the first. For three days before my birthday — in November 1981 — I couldn't sleep. This made me very tired and I became delirious enough to believe that the sleeping bag which I insisted on sleeping in on the floor of my room was the womb and I had gone back into it to be born again. There is hardly any point in my stressing again that I am not a religious person and I feel somewhat ashamed of these manifestations.

ELISH.   Then why tell me — why not speak with a doctor?

GRETA.   If I tell a doctor I am having religious visions, he will tell me that I am ill; and that is closure. If I tell a nun I am having religious visions then we can agree we are both ill and at least begin the conversation on an equal footing.

ELISH.   You are aware that I am Prioress here now?

GRETA.   I wasn't but I'm glad of it. For at least it means you have the spiritual authority to advise me. You see I don't intend being locked up for what one half of the world regards as an achievement of sanctity. My liberty is very important to me …
Also —

ELISH. Also?

GRETA. I haven't finished. I was aware during the experience of being in the womb on my birthday, my twenty-fourth birthday, that I could see out of two separate windows each with a different view. I felt very far down inside my own body. As I looked around the room, I saw an old man in the corner watching me. And I said to myself, I knew it. I knew that old man was there. I have felt watched all my life.

ELISH. It was the devil you saw.

GRETA. I knew that immediately. He looked like an old priest. *(Elish makes a movement.)* He was dressed like a priest in a long black soutane. He had a pointed beard. I must have been weak and small because I was looking around what I took to be the edge of a chair, a wing chair, or perhaps it was a pram hood. At any rate, the old priest loomed over me and placed a pillow on my face. I tried to cry out but he was smothering me. I was being silenced. And it was this I had to struggle against. I struggled against this smothering blackness until a voice said in my ear — a kind warm voice: "Turn round. You have to turn around." So I did, I turned myself around and found I could breathe again and ahead of me I could see this oh most beautiful globe, a sphere lit up in space far below me, and I found myself floating falling towards it. And the same voice, the one that told me to turn around, said: "Enjoy your fall through space and time." So I knew I was born that night. Or I was reliving my birth.

ELISH. And that was all?

GRETA. All? That was the beginning. Then the hair catching fire, then the flame in the curtain.

ELISH. Have you ever told anyone about this?

GRETA. Not a living soul — except my husband. I did tell him about the flame — when he came to pick me up from the cottage.

ELISH. What did he say?

GRETA. I was very stupid. I told him I'd seen a tongue of fire, and I discovered it was Pentecost Sunday. Stupid!

ELISH. What was his reaction?

GRETA. I lost him … He was repelled — what would you expect? He was a Marxist historian. He thought he'd found a radical secular emancipated woman, and instead he'd got a Catholic mystic.

ELISH. Then why did you tell him? You could have come to me then!

GRETA. I told him because I wanted him to talk me out of it, I suppose. But he didn't even try. Later my husband told me he was having an affair. We went away to try to talk about it. We were staying in a house in Exmoor. And I died.

ELISH. You died?

GRETA. And in my grief my voice left me. I experienced my own death.

ELISH. Why didn't you speak out before?

GRETA. I couldn't, I was afraid. I loved my husband and I had no context for dealing with this. So I shut it in another room and I lived in the outer room of my life I suppose. You see, after we came back from Exmoor, I deliberately got pregnant. So he couldn't leave me. That was what I did. That was my response!

ELISH. Why now? Why are you telling it now? Something has happened to make you speak out!

GRETA. Two nights ago at my sister's flat in London, a figure burst in on me. Stood there beseeching, wailing, shivering at the foot of my bed. I pretended it was a banshee. But it was no more a banshee than I am. We both know what I saw. Why are you crying?

ELISH. The light is hurting my eyes. Excuse me. *(She gets up to blow her nose and wipe her eyes.)*

GRETA. I kept it away for so long. I want to get this under control. Help me! You are crying.

ELISH. You should have been a nun.

GRETA. It's a bit late now. Have you any more practical advice?

ELISH. My mother was a woman of great sanctity. But instead of entering a convent which she ought to have done she married a worthless man with a handsome face who led her a merry dance.

GRETA. A merry dance? He tried to strangle her — was what

32

I was told.

ELISH. After I was born she went away to England, and I was left in the care of your mother. Until she got herself on her feet.

GRETA. On her feet? She got married again.

ELISH. A kind man who fell in love with her and proposed, before he knew about the baby in Belfast.

GRETA. And then you popped up.

ELISH. She told him she had a baby — me. And he still married her. So after ten months of marriage I was brought home to my mother in England. I'm supposed to look like him; the man who tried to strangle my mother. Did you know that? I'm his spitting image. I never really fitted in. And I was sent away to school. To be brought up by nuns. And I have been with nuns ever since. They didn't mind what I looked like — in fact my body wasn't important at all. I knew from the beginning this was how I would live, I felt safe and cared for. And I liked the order and the convent routine. I have strived for grace and revelation. I have followed every rule, I have read every text — and I love it here, don't misunderstand this — a convent is a republic of letters. I love the language, the structure, the ceremony, but I have never ever had a revelation such as you describe. I have fasted in Lent. I have lain awake for nights on end to achieve this state of grace that you so artlessly fall into. You and my mother share this — you are effortlessly and unconsciously almost always in a state of grace. They say that Mary Magdalene is the most sanctified woman in heaven. And I who have broken myself on the feet of the Redeemer — *(She indicates a purple-draped figure which is hanging above them in the hall.)* — am rewarded with this visit — and you ask me why I am crying? Did you come here to make fun of me?

GRETA. I have no wish to cast ridicule on your way of life, Elish.

ELISH. Bethany!

GRETA. I came here because I grant that your spiritual practices might give you some insight into my condition. I rather hoped you would open a door for me — which would allow me to live in the main room of my life. But I see I have only caused you distress, I'm sorry — *(Greta makes to leave. Elish blocks her path.)*

ELISH. I can talk to the archbishop, who is a friend of rnine.

GRETA. How can that help?

ELISH. You could take the sacrament of Reconcilation — and come back into the church.

GRETA. What is that? Reconcilation.

ELISH. Since Vatican Two it allows you be absolved provided you are prepared to meet a priest face to face and be confessed of your sins.

GRETA. I don't necessarily regard anything I have done as sinful I may have broken a few rules, that's all.

ELISH. These things that are happening to you are common in religious life. We just don't talk about them much. You see, the religious life offers protection for people like you. As you may now only enter religious life by rejoining your church I advise you to do so with some haste. I would like you to begin taking the sacraments again. Particularly Communion. You must receive the Host for your own protection. If you cannot be a nun in a convent at least you can be a nun in the community. We have a great many married women with large families who are our nuns in the community. The Mothers — they are the real harvesters of souls. You can be one of those.

GRETA. What exactly do I have to be protected from?

ELISH. You attract as much evil as you do good.

GRETA. That's terrible.

ELISH. You musn't think because I am in a convent that I am so safe or even more saintly. Or that I have good relations with all my sisters in this convent, far from it. I never go to bed without double bolting my door. I am surrounded by relics and crucifixes because I am afraid. I don't like sleeping in the dark. I even keep a luminous little figure of Our Lady of Lourdes under my pillow.

GRETA. Yes, I remember those little statues. They used to put them in our bedroom as children, luminous ones that lit up in the dark — I understood that it was to keep us from masturbating. Because you know you'd look up at the statue and think well I can't really do this — she's watching. It was clever.

ELISH. Och — you have been given a holy order, you are chosen, you have been spoken to directly but you are also chosen by evil as well. Nothing stands alone. Now if you come back to me tomorrow I will make arrangements for you to meet the archbishop or any other priest —

GRETA. Why a priest — why not you?

ELISH. I am not empowered.

GRETA. Because you are a woman?

ELISH. Yes.

GRETA. So — these men in skirts have usurped our function, don't you think?

ELISH. Perhaps in time this attitude of the church to women may change. After all, it took a long time before the Virgin Mary was given her rightful place in heaven. But it happened.

GRETA. Two thousand years is a long time.

ELISH. The Catholic Church changes slowly.

GRETA. I'm running out of time.

ELISH. You shouldn't let the rules stand in the way.

GRETA. Should I not?

ELISH. But you must abide by them; they are simply like a dam built to hold back the forces that will sweep you away.

GRETA. I am much afraid of going mad. If I thought joining the church would help me I would do it.

ELISH. Then you will come and see me tomorrow.

GRETA. I will come back, yes. Tomorrow. *(Elish is overjoyed, they embrace.)* But, if I am reconciled ... and I have Communion. What is my status as regards my husband?

ELISH. You can't be divorced.

GRETA. I can. I don't need the church's permission.

ELISH. You can't be divorced because you have never been married.

GRETA. I have a husband and three children.

ELISH. You have never been married in your soul.

GRETA. My God. You're defeating me with my own weapons. You're being metaphysical.

ELISH. You must be married to your husband in the church. Only that will bring you the peace of mind you desire.

GRETA. Peace — is it possible? But — if he refuses?

ELISH.   Then he is not your proper husband.

GRETA.   Good. Yes. That's very good. But my children? Wouldn't they be illegitimate?

ELISH.   They are not your children. They are God's children; they must be given back to him. You said yourself, you married in the outer chamber of your life. It is a long road — to reconcilation. But you know if you are reconciled then your children will follow. They must be baptized. *(Three bells are sounded.)* I am called to prayer. Will you come to see the Washing of the Feet? Will you not come? Today of all days?

GRETA.   It's not possible.

ELISH.   Then come tomorrow. Will you come tomorrow?

GRETA.   I must be going to the hospital.

ELISH.   I warn you if you decline to enter the church it is your own business. You may end up as a fortune-teller in a circus or a fairground. You may even make a living from it. It is when you go to meet your Creator that you will have to answer for the waste of such a spiritual gift.

GRETA.   I'm not afraid of death, you know. We have been companions for years. It's the living who have given me most trouble.

ELISH.   I fear for you terribly. *(Greta backs away.)*

GRETA.   No! Goodnight Elish — Bethany. Sister Bethany.

ELISH.   *(Calling.)* I'll remember you in my prayers. *(A large oak door is heard shutting. Elish stands before the purple-draped statue. She contemplates it. She drops her head and walks away.)*

SCENE 4

The Royal Victoria Hospital, Belfast. Later the same evening. A wide corridor. A bench between two sets of swing doors. The door on the right leads to the heart ward where Michael Flynn is lying. Rose Flynn enters. She is accompanied by her daughter Aoife.

ROSE.   *(Walking towards the bench outside the heart ward.)* I feel

36

terrible. He said: "I think I'm having a heart attack," and I laughed. I told him to go and lie down. He came back half an hour later and said, "I still feel sick, could you call the doctor." *(They get to the bench, Aoife plumps down on it but Rose remains standing.)* So I did: But even then I said: "Doctor, he *thinks* he's sick."

AOIFE. Sure you weren't to know.

ROSE. You blame me, don't you, you all blame me.

AOIFE. Och, Mammy, would you sit down, for God's sake. Nobody blames you. He's no one to blame but himself. Sure he's never at home. *(Rose sits.)*

ROSE. Helen blames me. She told me not to be talking to him about money. I don't talk to him about it. I never mention money.

AOIFE. Try not to worry —

ROSE. What's wrong with Greta? Have I done something on her? Did she say anything to you about me?

AOIFE. She's not too well.

ROSE. It's that husband, isn't it? There's trouble there. I never liked George. We weren't good enough for him. He wouldn't let the babies come to see us. What's wrong?

AOIFE. She's seeing things.

ROSE. Greta? What sort of things?

AOIFE. I'm not supposed to tell you this — you're not to repeat this — but the other night at Helen's flat she saw a banshee. It's probably only stress — you know.

ROSE. Are you kidding me?

AOIFE. No, I'm deadly serious.

ROSE. She's not on drugs, is she?

AOIFE. No. I was in the other room and I heard it too.

ROSE. They only cry for certain families. I didn't think we had one attached to us. Oh here, you don't think your daddy'll die!

AOIFE. *(Catching sight of Helen who is some way off, sweeping along the corridor towards them.)* Mammy, here's Helen, now don't let on I told you.

ROSE. *(Looks.)* Would you look at that; she's turned up here dressed to death. *(Helen sweeps on in a beautifully tailored suit and carrying a bunch of calla lilies. She is watched by the entire popula-tion of the corridor.)* For God's sake, do you always have to draw attention to yourself wherever you go. It's your daddy's day not yours.

HELEN.   Rise above it, Mother. Rise above the condition.

ROSE.   What's that supposed to mean?

HELEN.   You're angry because Daddy is ill — don't take it out on me.

ROSE.   Here, what's this about our Greta and a banshee?

HELEN.   Jesus, Aoife! Can you keep nothing from her!

ROSE.   I'm her mother. I have a right to know.

HELEN.   She's gone a bit religious.

ROSE.   So that's why she's gone to the convent. Then she re-ally is sick. For she was wild against religion. I couldn't get her to go to Mass after she was fourteen.

HELEN.   None of us went to Mass after we were fourteen. She was the only one who admitted it.

AOIFE.   That's true — our Greta was awful stupid. She always announced beforehand when she was going to break the rules.

ROSE.   Well she takes after that man in there. I haven't had a day's peace — for he's a born rebel!

HELEN.   Funny she even knew it was Lent. What was it, no milk?

ROSE.   I gave up the bingo.

AOIFE.   It's certainly strange to make a huge fuss about keep-ing Lent and her married to a Protestant and none of her chil-dren baptized.

ROSE.   Oh, they're baptized all right.

AOIFE.   They're not. She distinctly told me they weren't.

ROSE.   I can assure you they are. I took a cup of cold water one night and baptized them all Catholics.

HELEN.   When was this?

ROSE.   Och, one time they were over with me when they were small.

HELEN.   I call that an abuse of hospitality.

AOIFE.   Is that our Manus?

ROSE.   Oh God, would you look at the cut of him. *(Enter Manus, with a battered fiddle case.)*

MANUS. Sorry I'm late. I just got off the train from Portrush. *(He kisses them, one after the other.)*

ROSE. Och son, sure I could get you a good coat. You only have to say.

MANUS. I don't like coats. I'm all right. I was sleeping on a friend's floor.

HELEN. So you wore the sleeping bag!

MANUS. God, Helen, you look like a million dollars.

AOIFE. She is a million dollars.

ROSE. Stop it.

MANUS. Why don't you just wear your bank balance on your sleeve. *(She hits him.)*

HELEN. Lay off.

MANUS. How's the da?

ROSE. He's still breathing.

MANUS. Where's Madame Blavatsky?

HELEN. Who?

MANUS. Greta. *(Helen looks at him very curiously.)*

AOIFE. She was on her way — but I don't know what's happened to her.

ROSE. She went to the convent to see your cousin Elish and to take some clothes for the orphans from my shop.

MANUS. Oh yes. The clothes for the orphans — your conscience money.

ROSE. That'll do.

HELEN. Have you been drinking?

MANUS. Here, what's this about a banshee in your flat? *(Helen looks at Aoife who looks away.)*

HELEN. Aoife! *(To Manus.)* For God's sake don't let on to Greta you know.

MANUS. Sure I hear them all the time — usually when I've had a few.

AOIFE. *(Looking out along the corridor.)* She's coming.

ROSE. Listen you're not to mention Greta's problems to your daddy — you're not to say she's been in a mental hospital or that her husband has left her or that she won't get her children back. Or that he's had an affair.

HELEN. And we certainly won't mention the banshee. *(Greta*

arrives.)

GRETA. Hi. *(Kisses her brother, because this is the first time she's seen him.)*

ROSE. How did you get on?

GRETA. Fine.

ROSE. Did she like the clothes?

GRETA. Yes. They were great.

ROSE. What about the wee matinée jackets?

GRETA. Yes. She liked those as well.

ROSE. Did she ask after me?

GRETA. Yes. They're praying for my daddy.

ROSE. Oh, that's very nice of them.

GRETA. She seemed glad to see me. Gave me a cup of tea. *(A nurse, Emer McGillicuddy, holds open the plastic swing doors.)*

EMER. Mrs. Flynn, you can go in now. But you shouldn't all go in together.

ROSE. Thank you. Helen, you better come in with me. He was asking for you yesterday. *(They go in through the plastic doors. They leave Greta, Manus and Aoife alone.)*

AOIFE. Oh aye. Our Helen. The Lourdes Water. That's what he calls her.

MANUS. It's not that much of a compliment, since he doesn't believe in anything. So, how are you, kid?

GRETA. I'm grand. *(She heaves a tremendous sigh. The nurse comes out of the swing doors, and glances at Aoife. Emer McGillicuddy is wearing the red uniform of a staff nurse, with a white starched apron and a white crown cap on her head. The ordinary ward sisters wear blue and white. She has a country accent. Aoife looks up at her.)*

AOIFE. Emer McGillicuddy?

EMER. Aoife Flynn! Och, is that your daddy lying in there?

AOIFE. I was in Form Three with you.

MANUS. I'm off to have a pee. *(He exits.)*

EMER. I wouldn't have recognized your mammy, but you've not changed.

AOIFE. You always wanted to be a nurse.

EMER. Sure, it was the only way I could think of getting up to Belfast.

AOIFE. Do your family still go to the Dogs?

EMER. Oh yes. I have three or four greyhounds of my own now.

AOIFE. Do you make any money?

EMER. It's a business. You have to have some vices — sure you'd never know what good was.

AOIFE. And can you do the nursing as well?

EMER. I love it. I'm thinking of getting a transfer to maternity, though. It's the airport, isn't it. The airport for wee babies. I love the babies. They're the best.

AOIFE. None yourself?

EMER. No. Sure I wasn't good enough. My man didn't want babies. Then he married someone else and had them with her.

AOIFE. It has nothing to do with being good enough.

EMER. Isn't it?

AOIFE. No man wants babies. You have to be surreptitious about it.

EMER. My father walks past him in the street. You can't blame him. He rejected my father's grandchildren. He came in and out of our house for years; and he said no children. And then he ups and marries a woman from a good family and has three children with her.

AOIFE. Don't be daft! You come from a good family — you just get pregnant! You can do that — you're a nurse.

EMER. I'm going to find a man who wants my babies.

AOIFE. They'll run a mile first.

EMER. See you later. *(She walks off down the corridor and goes in the other visible set of swing doors — which connects with the heart ward.)*

AOIFE. That wee girl's not wise. Do you not remember her from school?

GRETA. Vaguely.

AOIFE. I wouldn't like to have her looking after me, if I was dying. *(The fiddle is heard playing in the distance — "The Harvest Home.")*

GRETA. Is he dying?

AOIFE. Of course not. I meant if I was dying. I didn't mean him. Mammy says it's only a wee shudder. *(Helen comes out of the swing doors behind her. She looks past her sisters.)* It's not a big at-

41

tack.

GRETA. Listen. I hear music.

HELEN. We all can hear music, Greta. *(Aoife gets up to confirm what she suspects.)*

AOIFE. *(Looking.)* Aye. It's our Manus. He's out there on the porch playing the fiddle.

HELEN. The fiddle? Manus?

GRETA. What's the name of the tune?

AOIFE. "The Harvest Home." I think. It's probably some woman he's after.

HELEN. He's gay.

GRETA. *(To herself.)* Oh God. It would be.

AOIFE. Och, that's just a phase he's going through.

GRETA. *(To herself.)* Home. Of course. This is the place.

HELEN. It's not, he's really gay.

AOIFE. I don't believe you.

HELEN. He turns up to my flat in London every so often with some little friend or other. Usually a musician. He had a girl-friend once — an American journalist — she was a complete ballbreaker. I was glad when he went back to being gay.

AOIFE. Och, he's probably neither one thing nor the other.

GRETA. I don't think Manus knows what he is yet. But when he finds out — he'll be very powerful.

AOIFE. He's young, that's all.

HELEN. Aoife, mammy says you're to go in now.

AOIFE. How is he? *(Helen shakes her head. Aoife goes in and Helen sits down and waits with Greta. Enter: Manus is playing the end of a reel, "The Harvest Home," on his fiddle. A woman patient in a pink quilted dressing gown does a slow dance, a reel. She'd be very pretty and poetic if she wasn't so roundly pregnant as well. Other patients in dressing gowns and night visitors to the hospital drift towards the fiddler and the girl. Suddenly she breaks the formation and runs across to Helen.)*

MELDA. Do you have a cigarette?

HELEN. No. And you shouldn't smoke in your condition. *(Manus goes on playing very softly.)*

MELDA. Oh look, there's a wee butt. *(She picks up a cigarette end from the floor and puts it in her pocket.)* I love the dances, don't

42

you?

HELEN. You dance very well.

MELDA. Don't you go to the dances?

HELEN. Not much. I'm too busy.

MELDA. I do. I love the Plaza. There's always a sailor. I'm very popular at the Plaza. You know why? *(Helen shakes her head.)* 'Cause my teeth light up in the dark. A sailor knocked them out once. And the new ones light up at the disco. See. *(She bares her teeth.)* Och, you need them funny lights to see them properly. *(Something else catches her attention.)* There's a lovely policeman. Maybe he'll have a wee butt. *(She darts off. Emer reappears.)*

EMER. *(Calling after her.)* Melda! Get away back on your own corridor and leave these people alone, there's a good girl.

HELEN. I didn't think they had the maternity wards along here. So near all this.

EMER. She's not from the maternity ward — she's from the banana ward.

HELEN. The banana ward?

EMER. She's nuts. She's down here every night chasing men. *(Helen looks after Melda.)* That's the third pregnancy in two years. They keep taking the babies off her.

GRETA. Why?

EMER. She's not fit to look after them. *(Some applause for the fiddler.)*

MALE VOICE. *(Off.)* Here, nurse, is that Fenian music never going to stop!

SECOND VOICE. *(Off.)* Play the "Ould Orange Flute!"

MANUS. *(Coming on.)* It's not Fenian, mister, it's Irish. It's your music. And I can play the "Ould Orange Flute" —

EMER. I really liked your playing, but I have to ask you not to do it again — some of our patients will be trying to sleep now. *(The crowd drifts away. Emer moves them all on.)*

HELEN. Since when did you play the fiddle?

MANUS. I wanted to get in touch with my own music for a change.

HELEN. You'll be taking us home to Glockamorra next.

MANUS. Glockamorra? Where's that then?

HELEN. I've never been myself — but I'm told it's where Irish

43

Americans go when they die. That's why you don't meet any of them in heaven.

MANUS.   Well, you've got nothing to fear.

HELEN.   Aren't we citizens of the world? We were the last time we met.

MANUS.   I don't feel like a citizen of the world when I'm treated like a Paddy and a Fenian git.

HELEN.   You don't have to stoop to other people's expectations. Don't descend to folk, compose something new.

MANUS.   The music grows in you like a tree and I can't compose something else until I know my own tree first.

HELEN.   Could you not rise above the tribe? Let there be one artist in the family.

MANUS.   All great art will have the tribe behind it.

HELEN.   Hopefully a long way.

MANUS.   What about yourself?

HELEN.   Let's just say I'm too commercial.

MANUS.   He robbed us, you know. My daddy. He brought us up like Protestants.

HELEN.   Well, my mother made up for it.

MANUS.   I'm talking about the music, the language, the culture. It was traditional, he said it was nationalist so we never learnt it. Now I spend all my time trying to get it back.

HELEN.   It was for the best. He didn't want us turning into rebels.

MANUS.   It was ignorance.

HELEN.   It made sense.

MANUS.   Not to me. *(Aoife comes out, she looks upset.)*

AOIFE.   He wants to be cremated.

MANUS.   What's the problem? Will he not wait till he's dead first?

HELEN.   Away on in you two and see your daddy. *(Manus goes in. Greta doesn't stir.)*

GRETA.   I will in a minute.

HELEN.   The visiting's nearly over. *(Aoife sits down.)*

AOIFE.   So what do you think?

HELEN.   What about?

AOIFE.   About Daddy? Was it a banshee? Do you think he's

44

going to die?

HELEN.   Probably.

AOIFE.   Do you not care?

HELEN.   He's been an invalid already for the past five years. I see a man in a wheelchair and a woman pushing him. I have a very complicated attitude to all this.

AOIFE.   What's that.

HELEN.   I hate it. I wish he were dead.

AOIFE.   God forgive you — you don't mean that.

HELEN.   I do. My mother is a prisoner of this!

AOIFE.   She'd be lonely without him.

HELEN.   Don't you believe it — she'd be off round the world. *(Greta gets up quickly and goes to the door of the ward.)* She's withdrawing from us, I'm worried.

AOIFE.   She's becoming very grand.

HELEN.   It's not that. She's too quiet. *(The doors open and Emer almost bumps into Greta. Helen stops Aoife from continuing.)*

EMER.   His mother even said to me, "Why did you never marry my Malachy?" I said, "I know." He's so unhappy with that woman — she's a real Queen Bee. Never lifts a finger. I baby-sit for them.

AOIFE.   Well, he chose her.

EMER.   You're right. No, you are. He did ... You know she can walk into a room and pick the most powerful person in it right away. There could be a hundred people in it. And she can find the most important person and go straight up to them.

AOIFE.   Then that was what he wanted.

EMER.   But once — before a big operation, we were just about to go into theatre and, he cried, and said: "Emer, she's pregnant, save me from this woman."

AOIFE.   And why didn't you?

EMER.   I don't know. I suppose I never really had that kind of courage.

AOIFE.   That's really sad — he loved you.

GRETA.   You have no bite.

EMER.   No bite?

GRETA.   Something crucial hasn't been aligned. *(Aoife gives Helen a large nudge.)*

45

EMER. You think I should see a dentist.

HELEN. It's not what she means. You don't have to say everything that comes into your head, Greta.

GRETA. I do. I can't help it.

EMER. Well, what do you mean?

GRETA. You can't finish something off. *(Emergency alarm bells. Emer leaps to her feet.)*

AOIFE. What is it?

HELEN. What's wrong?

EMER. I've got to go. *(She runs. She is soon followed by another nurse who comes through the double doors. Several doctors rush past. Rose comes out to look also.)*

ROSE. That's the emergency heart surgery bell. They rang that for your daddy.

AOIFE. They're coming in in bullet-proof jackets.

ROSE. There's been a shooting.

AOIFE. *(Looking.)* There's been more than one.

HELEN. Why so many armed policemen?

GRETA. Why so many?

ROSE. Because if it's an assassination they always send the police up to protect them. And they'd want to get a statement in case someone dies.

HELEN. Surely the gunmen wouldn't come into the hospital?

ROSE. Would they not? More likely they'd come in to finish them off. Especially if they were recognized. *(Helen gets to her feet. She walks a little way towards the direction she has been looking in.)*

HELEN. *(American.)* Excuse me.

PAUL. Hello. *(He is a uniformed policeman.)*

HELEN. *(Going closer.)* Can you tell me what's going on outside? I plan to drive home in a few minutes. Is it safe to leave the hospital just now?

PAUL. Where have you parked?

HELEN. About two cars from the entrance. Does it matter?

PAUL. Yes. Which entrance?

HELEN. Opposite the church. Why? *(Rose comes up.)*

ROSE. What's happening? We have to go home soon and they're still bringing people in on trolleys.

HELEN. It's all right, Mammy. I'm handling this.

PAUL. *(To Rose.)* Somebody went in and sprayed a pub on the Donegal Road. Nine dead. It's a retaliation for the betting shop.

ROSE. Ah God. Our ones.

HELEN. They aren't our ones! They have nothing to do with us. They are murdering bastards! *(Rose walks back to Aoife and Greta.)*

PAUL. Is that your mammy?

HELEN. It is.

PAUL. I thought you were American —

HELEN. I live in England. I've travelled around.

PAUL. A dolly mixture.

HELEN. I'm too old for dolly mixtures.

PAUL. Which way do you go home?

HELEN. North Belfast.

PAUL. You'll be all right getting home. That's if your car's still there.

HELEN. Could you explain to me why it wouldn't be?

PAUL. The army and police pass in joint patrols every fifteen minutes, outside the front of this hospital. Four vehicles: two police and two army. When the last vehicle passes the gangs move in. If you don't leave someone in your car it won't be there when you return.

HELEN. Thank you.

PAUL. My pleasure. *(He walks away. She walks calmly to the others.)*

HELEN. How come nobody mentioned the gangs?

ROSE. Sure how would we know, we've never been up here at night.

AOIFE. He's deliberately scaring you.

HELEN. He's succeeded. I'm worried about the car.

AOIFE. Your insurance will cover it — if it's not there we'll get a taxi home.

HELEN. *(Walking off.)* Go and say good night to Daddy, we're off in a minute.

ROSE. She's right. We ought to go. It's not good to be out late on this road. We better say good night to your daddy. And don't anybody mention the car or the betting shop or the shootings or —

AOIFE. We won't speak. OK? In fact we'll just wait here. You go and say good night. *(Rose goes into the ward.)* Are you all right?

GRETA. How many dead?

AOIFE. I think he said nine.

GRETA. Is this the Harvest?

AOIFE. Now calm down. We'll be out of here in a minute.

GRETA. Did I do this? Did I bring this death in here with me?

AOIFE. Oh, for God's sake stop it! *(Greta gets up.)* Where are you going?

GRETA. Away. Maybe if I go away it'll come with me and leave you all in peace.

AOIFE. *(Struggling with Greta.)* Helen! Helen! *(Helen's footsteps rush along the corridor towards then.)* We've got to get her home. *(Helen enters.)*

HELEN. More bad news.

AOIFE. Don't tell me — the car isn't there.

HELEN. No. The car's there. The windscreen isn't. *(Greta is tugging to get away.)*

GRETA. Let me go. It's my fault! I'm death, I tell you.

HELEN. There's a carpet of snow on the front seats.

AOIFE. It's snowing?

HELEN. No. It's raining — broken glass.

AOIFE. Greta! *(Greta rushes away along the corridor. Aoife chases her, followed by Helen.)*

SCENE 5

The following day.

A sunny yard behind the shop. Aoife and her mother Rose are winding wool. Aoife is holding out her hands and her mother is winding.

AOIFE. What's it for?

48

ROSE.   He's wants it for fishing.

AOIFE.   He'll not go fishing now.

ROSE.   That's what I say — but if I don't knit it, he'll think I've given up on him getting better.

AOIFE.   Even if he did get better, he'd fall down in the water if he caught anything worthwhile. He's not that steady on his feet.

ROSE.   I know. But you can't talk to him.

AOIFE.   It's very oily.

ROSE.   Sure it's best wool.

AOIFE.   Have you many to do? *(She nods at the box beside the chair.)*

ROSE.   Just what's in there.

AOIFE.   And business is good.

ROSE.   Och, it's always been my experience that money comes when you want it. And Easter's a good time for christenings. Then First Communion in May.

AOIFE.   So why are you sending the matinée jackets and christening bonnets back?

ROSE.   She's charging too much for them.

AOIFE.   But the work in them.

ROSE.   It's no good saying the work if people aren't going to pay her prices. Mrs. Mowen is a Protestant and her matinée jackets are machine knit but they're cheaper, and I can sell them faster than Cathleen's so I'm giving my order to her in future.

AOIFE.   You shouldn't send them all back. Keep a few, I still have the one she knit for the boys. Fifteen years ago.

ROSE.   *(Sigh.)* Is it that long? *(Helen comes around the side of the house; she has been out and is carrying car keys.)*

HELEN.   What are you doing sitting out here?

AOIFE.   That didn't take long.

ROSE.   I get all cooped up in the shop. And it's the first sunny day.

HELEN.   What happened to the grass?

ROSE.   I had it paved over — sure your daddy can't manage a garden and Manus is never home when you want him.

AOIFE.   No problems?

49

HELEN. I drove straight to the car hire firm and explained: I hired this car at the airport yesterday but unfortunately last night the windscreen got smashed and the stereo was stolen. The guy didn't bat an eyelid: "Where did you park?" he said. "Right outside the hospital, two cars from the front entrance," says I. Do you know what he said to me?

AOIFE. What?

HELEN. If I'd known you were going to the Royal I'd have given you an armoured car.

ROSE. It's that bad.

AOIFE. So what do we do tonight?

HELEN. Paul said we should take turns to sit in it.

AOIFE. Paul?

HELEN. The policeman who helped us last night was called Paul Watterson. Anyway I got a bright red Rover out of it. It's bigger than the one I paid to hire. They hadn't any small cars left. Go around the front and have a look at it.

AOIFE. I will in a minute. *(The phone rings inside the house.)*

ROSE. Away and answer that for me. It might be the hospital. *(Helen goes indoors.)* That wee nurse McGillicuddy said she'd ring. Awful nice girl.

AOIFE. Emer? I think she's got her eye on our Manus.

ROSE. My son? Tut. I thought she was too sweet to be wholesome. You know they're building a new primary school in the parish. I'd like the contract for the uniforms.

AOIFE. Do you have a chance?

ROSE. Doctor McCourt's niece is up for it too. But I said they've got all the other contracts, it's time it went to somebody else. And I've educated enough priests in this parish to found an order. So by rights it's my turn.

AOIFE. Why have you never had a contract for any of the schools before?

ROSE. Because every time I was up for one your father'd write a letter to the newspaper criticizing the church's attitude to integrated schools and that would be an end of it. The Mother Superior at the grammar school said to me once: "Mrs. Flynn, we could hardly ask you to supply the school uniform when your own husband doesn't believe in the existence of our

50

schools." I swear he did it on purpose.

AOIFE.   Why did you marry him?

ROSE.   What a question.

AOIFE.   Well, you disagree so much.

ROSE.   It wouldn't do for us all to be the same. *(Helen comes out and looks shocked.)*

AOIFE.   Daddy was the first Communist on the Falls Road, and you were a member of the Children of Mary. I mean, I don't expect people to be the same — but you weren't even close! *(Rose sees Helen's face. Aoife has to turn around to see her. Rose drops the hall of wool.)*

ROSE.   What is it? Is it your daddy?

HELEN.   Greta's been arrested.

ROSE.   Oh Sacred Heart, what for?

HELEN.   Theft.

ROSE.   My daughter a thief! Greta? I don't believe you.

AOIFE.   What did she do?

HELEN.   Some time this afternoon, Greta went to Clonard Monastery and took a chalice from a side altar during a Low Mass, and walked out with it, before anybody realized what was happening.

ROSE.   Oh Jesus Mary and Saint Joseph!

HELEN.   Then she took a bus to the city centre still holding the chalice.

ROSE.   Oh Sweet Jesus, have mercy —

HELEN.   It was full of communion wafers — which she began distributing —

AOIFE.   To the people in the bus queues.

HELEN.   Yes. All over the town. To anyone who would take them off her.

AOIFE.   She did it. She said she wasn't going to do it. Didn't she?

HELEN.   She did. And she did it.

ROSE.   What? You knew? You both knew? I can't believe this! I can't believe what you're telling me. You knew what she was going to do and you let her out on her own.

AOIFE.   She promised us she wouldn't.

ROSE.   So where is she now?

HELEN.   The police station.

ROSE.   For stealing a chalice?

HELEN.   They only wanted to be sure that it wasn't political.

ROSE.   Oh Mary Mother of God.

HELEN.   I told them that she'd been in a mental hospital in England and was out for a week because her daddy was in the Royal with heart trouble. So when I confirmed that she was just nuts they were happy to let her go

AOIFE.   Is she all right?

HELEN.   They said she was a bit dazed and was sitting holding the chalice like it was the Holy Grail.

AOIFE.   Och, God love her. I'd love to have seen it.

HELEN.   In England they lock her up if she's mad but let her go if she's political. In Ireland they lock her up if she's political and let her go if she's mad.

AOIFE.   Do you think Greta's mad?

HELEN.   No more than anyone else in this country.

ROSE.   And where is she now?

HELEN.   They said they'd let her go soon.

AOIFE.   The point is — it mustn't get out.

HELEN.   I know. If it gets in the papers we're done for.

ROSE.   You're done for! Catholics are being murdered in their beds in this area for less! You're done for!

AOIFE.   Were there any reporters?

HELEN.   Who knows.

AOIFE.   When does the early edition of the *Telegraph* get here?

ROSE.   What does it matter about the papers — the damage is done enough. I'll have the clergy down on me!

HELEN.   I managed to keep the police from ringing Doctor Campbell. But I can't guarantee to keep it out of the newspapers.

ROSE.   Who's Doctor Campbell?

HELEN.   He's her psychiatrist, in England. It might only be reported locally.

AOIFE.   That wouldn't be so bad.

ROSE.   Not so bad?

HELEN.   Look, Mammy, stop echoing everything we say. If Greta gets involved in any funny incidents, if she doesn't appear to be completely calm and sane, she won't get custody of her children.

ROSE.   Custody! She's not fit to look after herself, let alone children! I had no idea she was so ill. You'd no right to let her out on her own. I advise you to call a doctor immediately and get them to commit her; for I won't take responsibility —

HELEN.   I'm not calling a doctor here — they still issue electric shock therapy in this country, without the patient's consent.

ROSE.   My sister Clare had electric shock treatment. It didn't do her any harm. *(The gate creaks open.)*

GRETA.   I'm not ill.

ROSE.   How did you get up here so quickly?

GRETA.   I got a taxi. I didn't think you'd want a police car at the door.

ROSE.   You were worried about that after what you've done? God, you take the biscuit. You've done for me today, girl, I'm telling you.

GRETA.   Why, what's wrong —

ROSE.   I'm looking for the franchise for the school uniforms in this parish and you've just been arrested for stealing a chalice from the church. Wait till the parish priest hears about this!

GRETA.   They already know. They're not pressing charges. The Hosts weren't consecrated.

ROSE.   Well, that's something — it was just theft, not blasphemy! I'll be able to say that when my application comes up before the Board.

HELEN.   All you have to do is say Greta's ill.

GRETA.   I'm not ill. I acted deliberately. I keep telling everyone. And you told the police I was ill.

HELEN.   I did it to get you out. What did you think you were doing anyway?

AOIFE.   You said you wouldn't do it.

GRETA.   I suddenly understood it.

ROSE.   How could you? And your daddy in the hospital. No one is to tell him, right? No one is m mention it.

AOIFE.   If it gets into the paper of course — somebody's bound to mention it at the hospital.

53

HELEN.   Nobody's going to mention it at the hospital, don't be daft. *(Greta takes a piece of paper from her pocket.)* What's this? *(She hands Helen the piece of crumpled paper.)*

GRETA.   I issued a statement.

ROSE.   Oh my God, I think I'm going to join your father. *(She is clutching her heart.)*

HELEN.   Mother, stop it! *(Helen hands Greta back the paper.)* What did you say in your statement?

GRETA.   Read it.

HELEN.   No, you tell me.

AOIFE.   *(Snatching the paper.)* Oh, for God's sake! *(Reads.)* "It is rank hypocrisy of the churches in Ireland to condemn violence and to keep the schools apart. They must end separate education at once. We must have integrated schools for five-year-olds ..."

HELEN.   You criticized all the churches, then — not just the Catholic Church?

GRETA.   Of course.

HELEN.   Well, that's maybe OK.

ROSE.   Are you joking? You steal a chalice full of communion wafers from the altar and give them out around the town like confetti and then you make a statement criticizing religion in schools! I might as well close the shop ! Are you trying to put me out of business?

GRETA.   I don't give a toss about your business, Mother.

ROSE.   No, now you don't give a damn! You're a chip off the old block! You've got his perversity towards me!

GRETA.   Stop! Stop! Stop, Mammy. This is nothing to do with you.

ROSE.   The sooner you go back to England —

HELEN.   Greta, you mustn't do this. This thing — this is not your mission, love, please. You're not meant to act. You have to contain this voice that's whispering to you to do these things.

GRETA.   I feel compelled. I feel as if it were running away with me. The voice.

AOIFE.   Why did you do it, honey? You said to us you wouldn't?

GRETA.   I wanted to stop the killings. I thought if I obeyed the voice it would all stop.

HELEN. We have to go somewhere quiet.

GRETA. Am I sick then, Helen?

AOIFE. She doesn't look sick — she looks radiant.

HELEN. Sometimes very sensitive people are composed by the people around them, and if there's a lot of tension —

AOIFE. Maybe if you went to the coast tomorrow, a wee trip to the seaside.

HELEN. Why don't we all go — did you put your name on this statement when you issued it?

GRETA. Oh no. I'm not important. I'm just the vessel for the voice.

HELEN. Well, that's something. *(Sound of a car door slamming shut. Heavy boots running.)*

FIRST SOLDIER'S VOICE. *(Off.)* Halt!

MANUS'S VOICE. *(Off.)* I live here. *(Shouting.)* Ma! Ma! Will you come out here and tell these eejits, this is where I live!

ROSE. Och, what is it now — is there no peace? *(Rose is already on her feet and going forward as Manus edges into view, carrying a flat cardboard box [so he can't raise his hands]. He is being walked backwards at gun, or rather rifle, point.)*

MANUS. Ma! *(The First Soldier now comes into view, pointing his rifle at Manus. He is followed by another foot soldier. There is the occasional burst of radio sounds off as a large army vehicle is obviously parked close by. Rose gasps at the seriousness of the situation.)*

FIRST SOLDIER. You went through a road block, Paddy. *(The Second Soldier is covering the women in the yard with his rifle. They are stunned by this intrusion. Only Manus behaves as if nothing important was at stake.)*

MANUS. No I didn't. Your road block was in the middle of the road. I wasn't going to the middle of the road, I was coming in here.

ROSE. He does live here.

MANUS. And my name's not Paddy — Tommy.

FIRST SOLDIER. We'll have identification from you, Paddy *(Manus does not move. Helen steps forward.)*

HELEN. His name is Manus Flynn. 212 Collingwood Road, Belfast 14. *(She manages very quickly to produce her own driving licence from her bag.)* And my name is Helen Flynn, I'm his sister.

(She shows the Soldier her licence. He takes a good look at Helen standing in this Belfast backyard in her well-cut clothes, with her sisters.)

FIRST SOLDIER.   London?

HELEN.   Yes. That's right.

ROSE.   They're just over from England. At least these two are, but she's up from the country.

FIRST SOLDIER.   Where's your licence?

MANUS.   It's in the house.

AOIFE.   I'll go and get it for you if you like.

SECOND SOLDIER.   No one move.

ROSE.   He does live here, you see. He meant no harm. His daddy's in the hospital and — he was doing a wee message for me, to the wholesale and —

SECOND SOLDIER.   Get him to open the box.

FIRST SOLDIER.   Open the box, Paddy!

MANUS.   Not while you call me out of my name! *(Greta intervenes. She takes the box from his hands and opens it; it contains three white veils. She drops the box and holds the veils in her hands.)*

FIRST SOLDIER.   Somebody here getting married?

GRETA.   These are for children.

ROSE.   They're for wee girls. For First Communion.

AOIFE.   It's my mother's business. She owns the shop, she sells clothes for girls up to eleven.

ROSE.   Flynn's Outfitters, that's my business. *(Greta remains holding the veils in her arms. The Soldiers remain with their guns fixed on the people in the yard. The First Soldier is looking with curiosity and amusement at the scene. An Officer — who has clearly been on the vehicle radio — comes in quickly. He addresses Rose.)*

COMMANDING OFFICER.   *(He speaks quietly.)* Is this youth resident at this address, Madam?

ROSE.   Yes. He is my son, Manus Flynn.

COMMANDING OFFICER.   He left his car and rushed in here.

ROSE.   Well, this is where he lives. And he's on his lunch hour.

MANUS.   I've been stopped three times crossing the town.

COMMANDING OFFICER.   *(Persists in addressing Rose.)* It could have been an ambush for us. Or he might have been armed. We saw him hurry into this house and gave chase. It could even have been an attempt on the life of someone in this house.

56

ROSE. Yes. Fair enough. I do see how it looked to you.

MANUS. It's not fair. These guys were abusive to me before I got out of the car. They kept calling me thicko micko — that's why I walked into the house.

HELEN. That's enough, Manus. *(The Officer pulls the two Soldiers off.)*

FIRST SOLDIER. Have a nice day — Paddy.

AOIFE. *(Puts her hand on Manus's arm.)* Thank you, same to you. *(The Soldiers exit.)*

MANUS. *(Bursting out.)* Hogswash! Pigswill!

HELEN. Shut up!

AOIFE. I think I'm going to be sick. *(The sound of slamming vehicle doors.)*

MANUS. Down with Tudor England!

HELEN. Shut up, you stupid, stupid, person!

MANUS. Down with Troy!

GRETA. Stop it, please.

MANUS. Well, look at you lot — curtsy to the boys. I'm surprised you didn't offer them a cuppa tea, Ma!

HELEN. Selfish brat!

ROSE. Calm down. He doesn't know.

MANUS. Why is everybody treating me as if I've done something wrong.

HELEN. You left your car and rushed in here bringing the army in after you!

MANUS. I didn't know you were all out in the yard.

HELEN. Frig it! Look I'm trembling. *(Holds her hand in front of her.)* That officer just gave us three plausible reasons for shooting you. You defied a road block; you might have been armed; it might have been an ambush. The sort of thing you read about in the newspapers all the time. No one would have batted an eyelid in England.

MANUS. You're hysterical!

GRETA. We were in a backyard, Manus — they could have opened fire and asked questions afterwards.

AOIFE. And no one would know our story.

ROSE. When you're dead it doesn't matter.

GRETA. Because we wouldn't be alive to tell it. Do you

understand, Manus, all we have to do is stay alive and tell the truth.

MANUS.   I knew I'd be stopped today.

AOIFE.   Why?

MANUS.   Because of last night. We drew attention to ourselves when we went to the wrong place. I knew when we were standing there in the floodlights, beneath the wall and nobody coming out to us. I felt them watching.

GRETA.   It was eerie, the silence.

HELEN.   Well, I didn't know the police station was occupied by the army. I had to report the car.

AOIFE.   So we went to the wrong place — it's no crime.

ROSE.   I told you — you should have come home and rung them! They might have thought we were going to attack the barracks.

HELEN.   We'd hardly drive up to the front entrance and ring the bell.

ROSE.   There's a kamikaze element up here that would. Some of those fellas have nothing to lose.

MANUS.   I want to paint on the walls of all the police stations and army barracks: "Forget 1690! Forget history! Remember the pursuit of happiness is a Right of Man!"

HELEN.   I've seen those words on a wall somewhere else — and I wouldn't be alone in thinking it doesn't change anything.

MANUS.   It doesn't matter; it's the fact that the words are up there, it's a promise, a covenant of something. Otherwise they might get lost. Even if no one spoke them or they got painted over, it wouldn't matter, they'd come through again and again, they'd come through. So you have to do it — paint the words on the wall —

GRETA.   Sit down in the road!

MANUS.   Write them up there — before it's too late.

ROSE.   Och now, take it easy, son. Come on — I'll get your lunch or you will be late back to work. *(She goes towards the house.)* Here, Greta! Are you going to stand holding those veils the length of your arm? Put them away in the box in case they get dirty. *(Rose goes into the house. Manus remains in the yard.)*

AOIFE.   I nearly died laughing when you opened the box, and pulled out those tiny veils. That poor soldier must have thought — child brides! *(Greta puts a veil on her head.)*

GRETA. I do. I do. I do. *(Aoife takes another veil and trails it across the lower part of her face.)*

AOIFE. It's so mysterious.

GRETA. Helen? *(She hands her a veil.)*

HELEN. *(Touches it with her fingers.)* I wouldn't put it on — it might not be lucky. *(Greta removes the veil from her head.)*

GRETA. The soldiers came into the yard because I am meant to see these things. Because I am a tongue.

HELEN. Oh, now don't start down that road Greta!

MANUS. What road is that, Helen?

HELEN. She thinks she's a voice for the ancestral woes.

AOIFE. And why not?

HELEN. *(Looking into Greta's face.)* It was the Pleiades you saw not the Plough.

GRETA. Was it?

HELEN. The whole of Ireland is not crying out to you — it's your self! *(Suddenly a young man comes around the back of the house and into view.)*

PAUL. Helen?

HELEN. Paul!

AOIFE. Jesus, Helen — who's this?

HELEN. It's Paul Watterson. He helped us last night.

AOIFE. Oh, the policeman ... I didn't recognize you in your clothes —

HELEN. Come in. Come in. *(She leads him through the gate.)* The car's great — I got a new one.

PAUL. The army radioed an incident here. I was in Queen Street barracks when it came in. Is everything all right? I'm actually off duty but I thought I'd drop by.

HELEN. Fine — now.

AOIFE. It's not very nice having a conversation at gun point; it somehow doesn't seem equal.

PAUL. They were within their rights — your brother didn't stop at the road block.

AOIFE. He must have stopped — because he said they abused him before he got out of his car — they called him a thicko micko and I believe my brother. You tell him, Manus!

MANUS. I don't need to. He knows bloody rightly they abused me.

PAUL. They're a bit jumpy, that regiment — they've caused trouble all over the town today ... Some of those soldiers are over here with redundancy notices in their pockets.

AOIFE. It must be hard being married to a soldier. You know. When they're in a war that the government says isn't a war. In their minds it must be hard. You know, to go home and sit in pubs in Birmingham and London next to Irish people who they were told might murder them the night before. It must be hard to be an English soldier.

GRETA. It's the bombs in England, isn't it?

PAUL. Some of that regiment are from the town where the children were killed. *(Rose comes out into the yard.)*

ROSE. Would you like some tea —

PAUL. No thanks, Mrs. Flynn.

ROSE. A bit of sponge, maybe?

PAUL. Thanks, no —

ROSE. Son, your lunch is on the table.

GRETA. Are you a Catholic policeman?

PAUL. Aye.

GRETA. Then you know what it's like.

PAUL. What is it like?

GRETA. We have the faith of the killers and the guilt of the spared. *(Paul looks hard at her.)*

ROSE. *(To Manus.)* You'll be late back.

PAUL. Where are you working?

MANUS. Barman at the Stormont Hotel.

ROSE. He's got two jobs.

MANUS. I used to do a sixty-hour week but they cut it recently to twenty-three. So I work in a city centre pub in the afternoon.

PAUL. Listen, Manus — watch the old temper. Hmmn.

MANUS. A temper is a useful thing. I'm away on, Ma. See you at the hospital later. *(He goes into the house.)*

ROSE. Watch yourself.

HELEN. Thanks for coming to see how we were.

PAUL. How about a drink later. *(Helen touches his hand. They go out to the gate. She says something quietly and smiles. He leaves. Helen turns. They are all watching her silently.)*

HELEN.   He has no money and he's not married. I just want you to know.

AOIFE.   He's a policeman.

ROSE.   Just as long as you know his first loyalty won't be to you.

HELEN.   Are you kidding? I've just met a man who would die defending me.

AOIFE.   It's nothing personal, Helen — it's his job.

GRETA.   That's not the way to love.

HELEN.   Don't any of you come preaching to me about love.

ROSE.   No one in this family has ever gone out with a policeman before.

HELEN.   No, we've never been that respectable. *(A newspaper is thrown into the yard from a great distance.)*

BOY'S VOICE.   *(Off.)* Telly! *(The newspaper flies all over the yard.)*

ROSE.   That Bletherskite! I wish I could get my hands on him. He cycles past every night and fires the *Telegraph* at the back door, so it's been all over the yard when I get it. *(Helen picks it up.)*

AOIFE.   Well. Anything?

HELEN.   *(To Greta.)* You've been pushed off the front page by the abortion issue.

ROSE.   Terrible.

AOIFE.   Is that another girl who was raped in the Republic and wants an abortion in England?

ROSE.   Terrible.

AOIFE.   I think she should have the baby. This baby might be significant. I think if all the babies born of rape were allowed to be born — the world would be significantly different.

HELEN.   Yes, it would be worse — more unwanted and unloved children.

AOIFE.   No. I think it would be significant. How can you tell it would be worse?

GRETA.   You're completely crazy, do you know that?

HELEN.   Oh my God! There's a photo! *(They all crowd round.)*

AOIFE.   Any name?

GRETA.   What does it say?

HELEN.   England is a prison — I feel much better now that I've come back to Northern Ireland. Says: "Madwoman in bus queue." *(Pause.)* Just joking. It says: "Woman protests at Catholic Church's refusal to ordain woman priests!" *(She shows them the paper.)*

AOIFE.   I don't believe it.

GRETA.   Is that all? No mention of integrating schools?

HELEN.   Nothing. You have more escapes than Houdini, sister. *(Greta looks stunned.)*

GRETA.   So that's it. If a woman can be a priest, God can be female.

HELEN.   Who cares?

GRETA.   I care. It means that women might be loved.

HELEN.   Well, it's not going to happen quickly.

GRETA.   *(To herself.)* Then it doesn't matter what I say. It doesn't matter. Because whatever I do — it's what I do that counts. *(The telephone rings.)*

ROSE.   Get the phone, Aoife — it might be a customer. Helen will put people off with that English accent.

GRETA.   *(To herself.)* Because what I do has lots of meanings.

HELEN.   I don't have an English accent — I have an American accent.

ROSE.   Well, they'll think it's a wrong number and ring off.

GRETA.   *(To herself.)* And they decide what it means. Because they don't listen. And they don't look.

HELEN.   They? Who are you talking about? Who are they?

GRETA.   So I might as well stop speaking. I shall make no move whatever.

HELEN.   *(Alarmed by her obvious withdrawal.)* Don't be silly. It's only a bloody newspaper. Please, Greta, don't be like this. *(Aoife comes to the house door.)* We'll drive to the coast tomorrow and look at the seals —

AOIFE.   My daddy died. *(Greta screams: making the sound on stage that she made offstage in Scene 2 and was originally dissociated from.)*

ROSE.   Your daddy! He was my husband! *(Greta screams again. And screams: a beseeching wail.)*

HELEN.   *(Putting her hands to her ears.)* Stop that!

SCENE 6

The dining room: Michael Flynn's body is laid out in a coffin on the table. Greta is waking the body.

GRETA.   Funny how people who leave their own country stop living, in some part of themselves, in the same year in which they left. A man came to see me the other day. He left Mayo in '56, this man — and his clock stopped. Only he didn't know that it had. He'd been promoted on the railways, and he had to make a report at the end of every day. Just a brief note. A sort of memo of the numbers of trains and times and if anything unusual had been reported to him. But he couldn't write — and he thought if he told them they would sack him. So he copies the reports of all the other memos for previous years. As long as nothing unusual occurs he can go on copying. But he's afraid of being found out. And he will be found out. So I'm teaching him to write. And then again, a Hindu child came to me. He came to England from Nairobi when he was nine. He was sitting in the classroom on his first day at school and he copied the name of the person sitting next to him because he hadn't learnt to write. And for a long time no one noticed that he'd been writing somebody else's name, and it wasn't the name he was called at home. He didn't know what his own name looked like written down either. Somewhere along the line the link between sounds and words had been broken — lost. And by the time a teacher in another school picked up his book and said, "But that's not your name — that's a girl's name," the child was so confused they sent him to me ... Father, I recognize them, the man from Mayo and the Hindu child, because I am the same. I too am a copier. I do it out of fear. It was then I realized that we weren't the only ones: the man from Mayo, the Hindu child and me. I listen to people speaking and I hear that there are no individuals, only scattered phrases and competing ideas which people utter to bewildering effect all the time — *(Michael sits up in his coffin, he rubs his eyes.)*

MICHAEL.   Rose?

GRETA.   No, it's me.

MICHAEL.   Greta.

GRETA.   You haven't listened to a word I've been saying.

MICHAEL.   What about?

GRETA.   My anger. I was telling you that for a long time I was afraid, and then I tried not to be, and my anger came back and I let it in. And now I'm in even more trouble!

MICHAEL.   Trouble? Your mammy said you got into some trouble at school today. With the nun.

GRETA.   She called you a Communist. Daddy, what's a Communist?

MICHAEL.   I'm not a Communist — I just believe that the universe is democratic, that's all.

GRETA.   Democratic?

MICHAEL.   Everything equals everything else. I don't believe in hierarchies.

GRETA.   What's hierarchies?

MICHAEL.   You see — there are salmon in the rivers and there are minnows. And we say the salmon is king but sometimes it's better to be a minnow than a salmon.

GRETA.   When?

MICHAEL.   When you don't want to get caught. If there's a big net across the river it's easier for a minnow to get through.

GRETA.   *(To herself.)* I can't believe this. I have to believe that some things are more important than others. Or I can't act …

MICHAEL.   Just say to the nun, my daddy's not a Communist he's a democrat.

GRETA.   I can't.

MICHAEL.   Why not?

GRETA.   I've been expelled.

MICHAEL.   Good for you. That's the spirit.

GRETA.   She said, "You're not the sort of girl we want in this school." So I tried to pull off her veil.

MICHAEL.   That's the Dominicans for you. The worst things came out of Spain — Franco, the Inquisition, package tours!

GRETA.   She said I had a devil in me.

MICHAEL.   That wasn't the devil — that was your temper!

GRETA. That's just what I've been trying to tell you. Sometimes when I can't decide what to do, I get angry and find that I've already acted — my anger makes the decision for me. *(Hammering at the door. Rose is pounding the door with her fists.)*

MICHAEL. Is that woman starting up?

ROSE'S VOICE. *(Off.)* I can hear you. I know he's in there.

GRETA. What did you do to my mother?

MICHAEL. What did I do?

GRETA. You lived with a woman you didn't love for forty years!

MICHAEL. Sometimes commitment is more vital than passion.

GRETA. She knew you didn't love her.

MICHAEL. Love. Blather. Universal love is the thing. Love mankind. Love knowledge ... *(Sighs.)* At any rate I loved my children.

GRETA. I think I loved you too much.

MICHAEL. Come 'ere and tell me this — how are the twins? I would have liked to have seen them. You couldn't bring them over?

GRETA. Catherine went to Berlin with her orchestra and won fifty pounds playing poker on the train.

MICHAEL. She's a great girl, that.

GRETA. Nothing great about it — she's only eleven.

MICHAEL. And what about Joe?

GRETA. Oh Joe. Joe's a great fisherman. He made friends with the local farmer who let him fish his stretch of the river when he won't let members of the angling club fish there. He's a charmer.

MICHAEL. Who does he look like?

GRETA. He looks like you.

MICHAEL. He gets the fishing from me as well.

GRETA. Did I tell you how he caught his first salmon?

MICHAEL. I love that story. Tell me again.

GRETA. I couldn't believe my eyes when he produced it from the fertilizer bag hidden under bales of hay. He and the farmer decided it would be better to hide it so as not to cause jealousy with the locals, you know. Apparently he had worked it —

thought it was a small one until it jumped out of the water and when it came down it made such a splash he said you would have thought a full grown man had jumped out of the river sideways! *(Roars with laughter.)*

MICHAEL.   Just goes to show — there's no joy in privilege.

GRETA.   He got a bloody salmon.

MICHAEL.   But he couldn't tell anybody. It's all in the telling.

GRETA.   Oh, I don't know, it tasted pretty good to me. *(Rose hammering at the door.)*

ROSE'S VOICE.   *(Off.)* You love her more than you love me!

MICHAEL.   Is that poor woman starting up again? *(Begins to lie back in his coffin.)*

GRETA.   Don't go yet. Daddy, I made a terrible mistake.

MICHAEL.   It's your man — isn't it?

GRETA.   I don't know what to do. I don't know what to do.

MICHAEL.   I never liked him.

GRETA.   That's only because you couldn't dominate him.

MICHAEL.   Oh, he was an arrogant shite. I wish I'd hit him when I had the chance. Your mammy stopped me. "Don't hit him, Mickey," she said, "he'll sue you." I knew as soon as I looked at him. Peter Pan — the boy who never grew up, just grew old with that well-preserved face. Never understood why you threw yourself away on him.

GRETA.   I was afraid to be on my own ... I never go to bed without double bolting my door ... I don't like sleeping in the dark. *(Michael lies down finally.)*

MICHAEL.   I was having such a strange dream ... it was raining ... your mother and I used to fish in the rain ... she was a better fisherman than I was. *(Suddenly the door bursts open. Rose enters in her nightdress in great distress.)*

GRETA.   What is it, Mother?

ROSE.   Where is he? Where are you hiding him?

GRETA.   Here. He's just here. Come and look. *(Michael is lying in repose in his coffin. Rose kisses her husband's face.)*

ROSE.   There. That's the last kiss he'll get. My husband. Don't you go kissing him.

GRETA.   I won't.

ROSE.   Promise? I must be the last one to kiss him. Don't

chase my kiss away — will you?

GRETA. I won't. *(Rose strokes his face.)*

ROSE. He wants to be cremated.

GRETA. Yes.

ROSE. Do you think he'll feel anything? When the flames reach him.

GRETA. No.

ROSE. Just as well. The cemetery's full. The assassination victims are being buried on the edge of the car park. Of course you'd never know — except — you wonder why all the flowers are lying on the ground. *(Aoife comes into the room in her nightdress.)*

AOIFE. Are you still up, Mammy? Come back to bed.

ROSE. He wasn't inside a church for years. But you know he was a far better man than some of them that run to the altar on a Sunday morning.

GRETA. I know that.

AOIFE. *(Touches her father's hands.)* Sure he's a wee hero.

ROSE. Don't do that.

AOIFE. What?

ROSE. You mustn't be the last. I must be the last.

GRETA. Go back to bed. Both of you.

ROSE. No I'm staying here to watch my kiss, that nobody takes it. *(Helen and Manus come into the room.)*

HELEN. What is it?

GRETA. Mammy won't go to bed.

ROSE. I'll go if Aoife goes.

MANUS. Jeeze. Cats and dogs!

AOIFE. He was my daddy. I can touch him if I like. *(She goes over to kiss him. Rose pushes her away.)*

ROSE. He's my husband. Not yours!

AOIFE. I'm his daughter. You're only his wife.

ROSE. Only his wife! What are you saying?

AOIFE. We're his blood love, not you!

HELEN. Aoife!

AOIFE. And blood love is stronger.

ROSE. I'm your mother.

AOIFE. Not much of that either.

67

HELEN. Aoife, stop it.

AOIFE. He was both a mother and a father to me!

GRETA. Manus — get her out of here. Now!

MANUS. No.

GRETA. Helen! *(Helen goes to Aoife and Greta gets hold of her mother.)*

AOIFE. You never loved your children, Mother. You never loved your daughters. You hated us every last one. You only cared for your son. You tried to turn our father against us. *(Rose almost collapses under the strain of this harangue. She gasps and clutches her heart. Helen tries to drag Aoife to the door.)*

HELEN. You're killing your mother. Will you stop it.

MANUS. It's true. Every word Aoife says is true. *(Rose turns to him.)*

ROSE. Oh son, son. Not you as well. *(He holds up his hands, to prevent her from embracing him.)*

MANUS. Don't — touch me! Woman! *(Rose turns again.)*

ROSE. Greta, you tell them. You took care of me when I was sick. You tell them.

MANUS. Aye, Greta, you tell us. How you really believe that she worried him into an early grave with her grubby till and her money problems.

GRETA. Manus, you are vile.

MANUS. Sure I am. But then I'm the money-lender's son!

ROSE. But I kept you. I educated you. We came up from the country with nothing and your father couldn't get work and I started knitting and then I did dressmaking and I made my money fairly and squarely. And when they couldn't pay I lent them the money. There's nothing wrong with that. I paid for your music lessons. Remember that.

MANUS. My father thought there was something wrong with it.

ROSE. He was unrealistic.

MANUS. He wasn't unrealistic; he was ashamed! I mean, you had a captive community here, didn't you. No communion dress, no First Communion. It was either a new communion dress or damnation and your interest rates stood between them and their souls.

ROSE. I did it for you. I did it for all of you. I suffered, don't think I didn't suffer. You tell them, Greta. How I was sick for a kind word.

GRETA. She did. She really did. She lost him. I was the one who had to pick her off the bathroom floor where she was lying drunk? No one but me to hold up her head.

MANUS. And what about the batterings she gave me?

GRETA. You? What are you talking about?

ROSE. I didn't know what I was doing. I didn't know what I was doing.

GRETA. Leave her alone!

MANUS. She drove you into the ground and you're standing up for her.

ROSE. My children hate me. My children hate me.

HELEN. I'm sick of this — what did you call it, Aoife? — blood love.

AOIFE. We are his children, she is only his wife.

HELEN. There's her blood in us too.

AOIFE. But there's more of his, and he was a better person.

HELEN. If he was better, it was because she enabled him to be.

AOIFE. *(To Helen.)* You're wearing his sweater.

HELEN. I was cold. I put it over my nightdress.

ROSE. Give me that, it's mine.

HELEN. All right. Here. *(Helen removes the sweater. She has a thin silk tunic underneath. Rose had not intended to expose her daughter's nakedness and turns in confusion.)*

GRETA. Give Helen back the sweater; she'll get cold.

ROSE. Where did you get this, huh? I locked his clothes away.

AOIFE. He left his clothes to me. They're for Damion. Helen can't have them.

GRETA. Not even an old sweater? Just to borrow?

ROSE. What are you asking her for? I'm the wife here. No-body gets anything without my say-so.

GRETA. Can Helen borrow the sweater?

HELEN. I don't want it. *(Greta gently takes it from her mother. She gives it back to Helen.)*

GRETA. It makes me cold to look at you. *(Helen takes the*

69

sweater.)

HELEN.   Here, Aoife. For you. So you can fuck your husband in your father's sweater. *(Helen exits. Manus picks up his violin. He mimes playing but makes no sound.)*

GRETA.   What are you doing?

MANUS.   I'm trying very hard to compose myself. *(Aoife puts on her father's fishing sweater.)*

AOIFE.   I'm sorry, Mammy.

ROSE.   People don't mean what they're saying half the time. You shouldn't take any notice.

MANUS.   Here lies a man who lied ... Silent father, huh? Silent?

ROSE.   I'm so tired. I'm so tired ...

AOIFE.   He's not gone. He's right here with us ... I'm happy. I'm really happy.

ROSE.   Would anyone like some tea ... I've made tea.

GRETA.   How did he lie?

MANUS.   God, Greta. You are so naive.

GRETA.   It's no disgrace. *(They all exit, leaving Greta alone. She leans over the coffin.)* Are you in heaven, Father? What's it like? *(Michael's hand comes up out of the coffin and grabs her by the throat. She struggles to free herself. She fights it off. Gasping, she drops to her knees on the floor. A cup is rattling in a saucer. Helen, who has put on her clothes, approaches carrying the cup of tea.)*

HELEN.   *(Gently.)* Are you all right?

GRETA.   I was dreaming ... it was raining.

HELEN.   It is raining. Look. *(Greta has taken the cup of tea from her. Helen goes to the window.)* What does that mean — when the outside and the inside are the same, I wonder?

GRETA.   They used to go fishing in the rain. My God! *(She drops the cup.)* He really loved her! *(She addresses him.)* You loved her more than you loved me! I took all those batterings because I thought that ... you loved her even though she beat me ... my God! *(Helen comes over to hold her sister.)* I thought I deserved them!

HELEN.   *(Shaking her head.)* It's over, Greta. Forget it.

GRETA.   Let's get away from here. I want to go home. *(Aoife comes in.)*

AOIFE.   When are you two going?

HELEN.   Tomorrow, after the ceremony.

AOIFE.   What shall we do with the ashes?

GRETA.   Chuck 'em in the Bann.

HELEN.   Feed him to the eels at Toombridge.

AOIFE.   Aye, right enough. He was a fisherman; he'd appreciate that. *(Manus returns.)*

MANUS.   It wasn't her fault, you know, my mother.

GRETA.   How did he lie?

MANUS.   He was afraid to speak —

GRETA.   Afraid? Father! He led the fishermen into a dispute with the eel fisheries which cost him his livelihood. He wrote to the newspapers attacking the church, so no Catholic would employ him! He was the bravest, most outspoken critic —

MANUS.   He was afraid to speak to my mother! So he talked to us instead.

GRETA.   But why did she beat us and not the others?

HELEN.   Because you said everything he felt.

AOIFE.   It wasn't that. It was because you two looked more like my daddy. She used to call him Kate. Then she'd say *(Pointing to Greta.)* DupliKate and TripliKate *(Pointing to Manus. They laugh. The door opens.)* Oh, hi Mammy, still up? *(Rose stands looking at them.)*

ROSE.   Don't stay in here too late. You never know who that light will attract.

MANUS.   Ah, we'll be all right.

ROSE.   There was a woman further up the road — she heard a noise and went to the window and looked out — she was —

GRETA.   Don't say it, Mother. It'll happen if you say it!

ROSE.   No. I was only going to tell you about —

HELEN.   All right.

ROSE.   I'm going to bed. Night. Night. *(The door closes.)*

MANUS.   *(Quietly.)* It wasn't her fault.

AOIFE.   She never got over losing the land.

MANUS.   An acre of stony ground.

AOIFE.   All the same. They were forced out.

HELEN.   Are there any Catholics left there?

MANUS.   They were on the wrong side of the river for

Catholics.

AOIFE. People warned him about that house. It kept changing hands in the twenties and thirties. But m'daddy took a loan and bought it when they first married.

MANUS. It was very cheap. That's what I heard.

HELEN. How come you can live there?

AOIFE. Damion's mother's been there for three hundred years. *(Manus sniggers.)* I know. She looks it. Daddy missed that river when they moved.

GRETA. I know he did. I know he did.

AOIFE. Why did they stay together? A Catholic and a Communist.

HELEN. Us, maybe.

MANUS. What are you talking about? Sounds a fairly normal combination for most European countries.

GRETA. Why has it never inhibited you — being a Catholic, Aoife?

AOIFE. Inhibited me? Why should it?

GRETA. You have affairs and you still go to Mass.

AOIFE. I don't have affairs — I have phone numbers. I fail to have affairs. Mostly.

GRETA. But you have no guilt. You would if you could get away with it?

AOIFE. Sure.

GRETA. What do you tell the priest in confession?

AOIFE. In the end it's between me and God. And if He doesn't mind it's nobody else's business.

GRETA. How do you know He doesn't mind?

AOIFE. I just say, "I know I'm married to you, God, but would you mind if I had a wee fling with So and So?" *(A whistling is heard outside the window. It is not tuneful. Only Helen and Manus will hear it first time.)*

GRETA. How do you know if He says yes?

AOIFE. If it happens, it was yes. If it doesn't, it was no. *(A whistle again.)*

HELEN. Listen.

MANUS. Is someone out there?

HELEN. Get away from that window!

GRETA. Get the light! *(She means put it out. Manus turns out the light. Darkness. The door opens, throwing light from the hall across the dark floor. Rose enters with a candle.)*

ROSE. Get down, children, under the table. If the windows come in you'll be cut to pieces. *(Rose gets under the table. They all watch in disbelief.)* Now isn't this nice. Who's going to tell us a story?

GRETA. Shouldn't we — [go into the other room?]

HELEN. This is ridiculous. There's no way I'm getting under the table. *(A foot kicks over some bottles.)*

MANUS. There is someone out there. *(Sound of shots firing outside. They all dive under the table with Rose.)*

HELEN. Do you think we should keep a bucket of water handy?

ROSE. Why?

HELEN. In case of fires starting?

ROSE. Sand would be better.

HELEN. We don't have sand.

GRETA. I think we should all stay downstairs tonight.

AOIFE. I think we should all sleep with our knickers on.

MANUS. I won't sleep. I'll keep watch. I'll sleep tomorrow.

GRETA. Suddenly — tomorrow seems very important to me.

MANUS. I'm sorry, Mother.

ROSE. It's all right, son.

MANUS. You know I'm never going to get married.

ROSE. I know. *(Another shot is fired outside.)* It'll be morning soon. Don't worry.

AOIFE. You know, this table isn't as solid as it looks. There's light passing through it all the time. Only we can't see it.

GRETA. Who told you that?

AOIFE. I met a lovely man called Roger Armstrong on my very first day at university. He's a scientist and he explained all about the table.

GRETA. Did you not love him, Aoife?

AOIFE. He was from the Lower Bann, just near where we grew up —

ROSE. There are no Catholics on that part of the river.

AOIFE. Roger's a scientist — he doesn't care about religion.

ROSE. But the family —

GRETA. — funny how you never get away from it.

ROSE. Masons. The Armstrongs. Orangemen.

HELEN. You have to go away to get away.

MANUS. No you don't. You can stay and get away.

GRETA. If I get away this time, I'm never coming back.

ROSE. This is nice, isn't it. We're all together again.

AOIFE. I mean it wasn't really anything to do with that, but once I read him a poem I'd written — about a kiss — it was called Corpuscles of Love. And he laughed. Roger Armstrong laughed at me.

HELEN. Corpuscles of Love?

AOIFE. So I decided, right — not him! Damion never laughed.

GRETA. Did he read the poem too?

AOIFE. Yes. He thought it was wonderful. He kept saying Corpuscles of Love, Aoife? Corpuscles! And then he kissed me. And I never let boys kiss me in those days until the third date. And Damion kissed me on the second.

GRETA. I suddenly feel very insecure about the table.

HELEN. I think we should move from here while it's quiet. We should go into the other room. Just in case.

GRETA. I think so too.

MANUS. Come on, Mammy.

ROSE. You lead the way, son. *(He takes Rose's hand and leads her through the dark with the flickering candle into the lit doorway. The others follow. Aoife remains in the lit doorway for a moment and then closes the door.)*

SCENE 7

Westminster Bridge. Just before 5 A.M. One week after Michael Flynn's death. A stone seat in the wall.

Helen walks towards the stone seat. She has a brown paper bag with two bottles. One of orange juice and the other, tequila. Greta walks on. She has the remainder of her father's ashes in a small plastic bag.

HELEN.   Over here! Come on. *(Helen plumps down on the seat.)*

GRETA.   Nobody sleeping on it?

HELEN.   We've had an awful lot to drink.

GRETA.   What time is it?

HELEN.   Quarter before five.

GRETA.   Triceratops and diplodocus don't get on, did you know that?

HELEN.   No. *(She takes a swig of tequila.)* I didn't. What?

GRETA.   Dinosaurs. My daughter told me that, once. Fucking dinosaurs! *(Greta gets up on the seat and up on the wall as Helen raises the bottle of orange juice to her lips.)*

HELEN.   *(Suddenly alarmed.)* What are you doing?

GRETA.   Scattering the ashes.

HELEN.   You don't have to do it from here — I thought we could go down to the edge with them.

GRETA.   No, it's better from here, the wind will carry them far.

HELEN.   What wind? *(Greta is now standing on the top of the bridge.)*

GRETA.   Earth has not anything to show more fair — than the new MI6 building over there. *(She tosses into the Thames some of her father's dust.)* Dull would he be of soul who could pass by a sight so touching — as the homeless on Westminster Bridge. *(She scatters more ashes.)*

HELEN.   I still think we should have chucked them all in the Bann. He won't like being divided up.

GRETA.   The city *now* doth like a garment wear — *(Sound of horse hooves on the road coming towards them.)* The police cars in Trafalgar Square, the soldiers in the hedgerows by the House of Commons. *(Sound of hooves gets closer.)*

HELEN.   Greta, hurry up and get down.

GRETA.   Silent bare — ships, towers, domes, theatres and temples lie open unto the Irish. *(Helen looks anxiously at the approaching riders.)*

HELEN.   We are attracting the attention of the mounted police.

GRETA. Wordsworth, your country needs you!

HELEN. They'll think we're up to something. *(Helen waves at the passing hooves which are very loud as they are now directly opposite the two women. Even Greta turns.)* Hi. Celebrating.

POLICEMAN'S VOICE. *(Off.)* Don't jump, will you?

HELEN. We're getting married tomorrow. *(She lifts the bottle of tequila.)* Cheers. *(The hooves pass on.)*

GRETA. Words! So do I cast out all devils!

HELEN. Greta, please get down now. *(Greta hesitates for a moment.)*

GRETA. Aye — I can't.

HELEN. Take my hand. Please take my hand. *(She climbs on to the stone seat.)*

GRETA. I can't.

HELEN. Greta, why are you doing this — I thought you were better. Glad to be going home.

GRETA. I can't live without my children. And I can't live with George. And I can't live here any longer and I can't — I can't —

HELEN. Greta, it's not just him. It's me. I'm doing this to you.

GRETA. No.

HELEN. Yes. I've always done this to you. I'm your opposite and I won't let you change into what it is you want to become. You want to be an artist and I won't let you because I'm the artist in the family. You want to be a beautiful woman and I won't let you because I've always been the beautiful woman in the family. You want to be late and you can't be because I've always been the last one through the door.

GRETA. No.

HELEN. Yes. Get down off the fucking wall! *(She grabs her hand and holds on.)* Or take me with you, honey! Why are you doing this to me?

GRETA. I can't help —

HELEN. He's dead. Let him go. Our father is trying to drag you into that river after him — let him go! Don't rot the lives of your children on his account! Your family love you and I know you love that man. Don't break up your little family out of pride. I'm saying this for me too. I wish I had a family. I wish

76

I had children. I wish — *(Greta gets down calmly and sits beside her.)* I could hit you.

GRETA.   I'm sorry. *(She embraces her, both of them struggling with tears.)*

HELEN.   He wouldn't let go of me either. So I had my revenge on my socialist father. I became a capitalist in the most intimate sense: I only come if there's money.

GRETA.   God, Helen!

HELEN.   That wasn't the worst thing I did. I'm not guilty about the money. I fed a lot of starving children. I may even have educated a few nuns.

GRETA.   The orphanage. You sent Elish money.

HELEN.   I did. No, the worst thing I did was to squander a great gift. I took my gift, which was very powerful and I used that power to seduce and dominate. When I should have used that power to create and free.

GRETA.   What will you do?

HELEN.   Start by selling my place.

GRETA.   Do you have to sell it?

HELEN.   I don't want to live like this any more. Anyway — you spooked me, you cow. You and that bloody banshee.

GRETA.   But you don't believe in it.

HELEN.   About this much of me does. *(Thumb and forefinger.)* There was something I didn't tell you — but on the night after we got back from Ireland I had to go out, if you remember. At first I was calm — I'm the cold one in the family, I'm not supposed to get upset — it was only later when I drove home I shut my thumb in the car door. Because I was so numb with grief I couldn't feel the edges of my own body. Well, that brought me back to my self I can tell you. *(She stares at her dark thumb.)* So I spent the night with my thumb in a bag of ice, and it was this, I think — the fact that I couldn't really sleep properly because the ice would melt and the pain would come sharply back and that would waken me, I'd have to go off to the fridge for more ice, so I slept badly ... Somewhere around 5 A.M. the pain returned again ... I opened my eyes and I noticed it ...

GRETA.   What did you see?

HELEN.   ... Wings and eyes of light were falling through the

77

rooms. Swirling and falling and gathering, passing through the roof and walls. And it's there all the time. Like Aoife said. I believe it's there all the time.

GRETA.   And then?

HELEN.   I fell asleep. I was exhausted. And when I woke up later I couldn't see it any more.

GRETA.   Well maybe you shouldn't sell it — your apartment — you know. Maybe it's a magical place.

HELEN.   No, the place is inside me. I carry it wherever I go. And so do you.

GRETA.   Yes. I do.

HELEN.   Sometimes when I'm out of my normal environment or someone takes me by surprise, or I wake up before I've finished dreaming, I forget for a moment what it is I'm supposed to see and that's when I achieve it. That's when I come closest, when I grasp the possibilities before the walls or the rooms I'm supposed to see assert themselves.

GRETA.   Yes. *(Suddenly reacting to a sound.)*

HELEN.   It's my memory that stops me from seeing. So I'm concentrating on forgetting —

GRETA.   Listen, can you hear that baby? Listen! Where could a baby be at this time of the morning? And so near? *(Big Ben strikes five.)*

HELEN.   That's not a baby, that's a clock.

GRETA.   No, I've got a baby's voice in my ear — oh dear. I'm doing it again, aren't I?

HELEN.   It's not saying anything religious, is it?

GRETA.   Oh no. It's just a baby — laughing.

HELEN.   Time you went home.

GRETA.   Yeah. I think so too.

HELEN.   I hope you have a good time, Greta. You need it.

GRETA.   I hope too.

HELEN.   And I hope it lasts.

GRETA.   Nothing lasts. But I'd like it to be good for a while, just long enough for me to get my strength back. *(Helen is suddenly on the brink of tears.)*

HELEN.   *(Recovering.)* Look how far the sun has come up since

we've been here. *(They both sit looking at the sun rising in the east.)*
GRETA.   You know — I'm very hungry.
HELEN.   Breakfast?
GRETA.   Breakfast. *(Exit. A baby is laughing. Echoes.)*

SCENE 8

Greta is at home, rocking a baby, telling it a story. The traditional empty chair is placed near the storyteller.

GRETA.   After Easter we came to the place. It was snowing in the forest and very cold into the fifth month. My mother and I were hunting. But because of the cold we couldn't feel anything or find anything to eat. So we sat down by the stream. I looked up and saw it suddenly, a stag, antlered and black, profiled against the sky. It stood on a ridge. This stag was from the cold north. It leapt off the ridge and down into the stream. It leapt through hundreds of years to reach us. And arrived gigantic in the stream. My mother was afraid, but I saw that it was only hungry. I took some berries from my bag and fed the stag from the palm of my hand. The stag's face was frozen and I had to be careful because it wanted to kiss me, and if I had let it, I would have died of cold. But gradually as it ate, its face was transformed and it began to take on human features. And then the thaw set in I could hear the stream running, and the snow began to melt. I could hear all the waters of the forest rushing and it filled my years with a tremendous sound. *(Pause.)* So I got on the stag's back and flew with it to the top of the world. And he took me to the place where the rivers come from, where you come from ... and he took me to the place where the rivers come from, where you come from ... and this is my own story.

HARVEST HOME
(as played by MANUS in Scene 4)

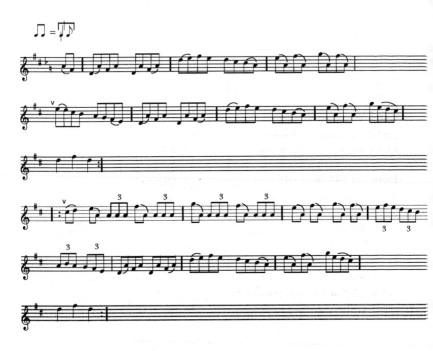

Trad.

Fiddle

PROPERTY LIST

Overnight bag (YOUNG WOMAN)
Glass of white wine (HELEN)
Glass of water and pain killers (HELEN)
Bundle of clothes in brown bag (GRETA)
Tea trolley (NUN)
Calla lilies (HELEN)
Battered fiddle case (MANUS)
Fiddle (MANUS)
Ball of wool (ROSE, AOIFE)
Car keys (HELEN)
Piece of paper (GRETA)
Flat cardboard box filled with tiny confirmation
    veils (MANUS)
Rifle (FIRST SOLDIER, SECOND SOLDIER)
Driver's license (HELEN)
Newspaper (thrown onstage by BOY)
Cup of tea (HELEN)
Candle (ROSE)
Brown paper bag with bottle of orange juice and
    bottle of tequile (HELEN)
Ashes in plastic bag (GRETA)

SOUND EFFECTS

Bloodcurdling wail
Phone ringing
3 bells sounding
Large oak door shutting
Emergency alarm bells
Footsteps
Gate creaking open
Car door slamming
Heavy boots running
Radio sounds from army vehicle
Slamming vehicle doors
Boy's voice
Hammering on the door
Whistling
Foot kicking over bottle
Shots firing
Horse hooves
Big Ben striking five
Baby laughing

NEW PLAYS

• **SMASH by Jeffrey Hatcher.** Based on the novel, AN UNSOCIAL SOCIALIST by George Bernard Shaw, the story centers on a millionaire Socialist who leaves his bride on their wedding day because he fears his passion for her will get in the way of his plans to overthrow the British government. *"SMASH is witty, cunning, intelligent, and skillful."* –Seattle Weekly. *"SMASH is a wonderfully high-style British comedy of manners that evokes the world of Shaw's high-minded heroes and heroines, but shaped by a post modern sensibility."* –Seattle Herald. [5M, 5W] ISBN: 0-8222-1553-5

• **PRIVATE EYES by Steven Dietz.** A comedy of suspicion in which nothing is ever quite what it seems. *"Steven Dietz's ... Pirandellian smooch to the mercurial nature of theatrical illusion and romantic truth, Dietz's spiraling structure and breathless pacing provide enough of an oxygen rush to revive any moribund audience member ... Dietz's mastery of playmaking ... is cause for kudos."* –The Village Voice. *"The cleverest and most artful piece presented at the 21st annual [Humana] festival was PRIVATE EYES by writer-director Steven Dietz."* –The Chicago Tribune. [3M, 2W] ISBN: 0-8222-1619-1

• **DIMLY PERCEIVED THREATS TO THE SYSTEM by Jon Klein.** Reality and fantasy overlap with hilarious results as this unforgettable family attempts to survive the nineties. *"Here's a play whose point about fractured families goes to the heart, mind -- and ears."* –The Washington Post. *" ... an end-of-the millennium comedy about a family on the verge of a nervous breakdown ... Trenchant and hilarious ... "* –The Baltimore Sun. [2M, 4W] ISBN: 0-8222-1677-9

• **HONOUR by Joanna Murray-Smith.** In a series of intense confrontations, a wife, husband, lover and daughter negotiate the forces of passion, lust, history, responsibility and honour. *"Tight, crackling dialogue (usually played out in punchy verbal duels) captures characters unable to deal with emotions ... Murray-Smith effectively places her characters in situations that strip away pretense."* –Variety. *"HONOUR might just capture a few honors of its own."* –Time Out Magazine. [1M, 3W] ISBN: 0-8222-1683-3

• **NINE ARMENIANS by Leslie Ayvazian.** A revealing portrait of three generations of an Armenian-American family. *" ... Ayvazian's obvious personal exploration ... is evocative, and her picture of an American Life colored nostalgically by an increasingly alien ethnic tradition, is persuasively embedded into a script of a certain supple grace ... "* –The NY Post. *"... NINE ARMENIANS is a warm, likable work that benefits from ... Ayvazian's clear-headed insight into the dynamics of a close-knit family ... "* –Variety. [5M, 5W] ISBN: 0-8222-1602-7

• **PSYCHOPATHIA SEXUALIS by John Patrick Shanley.** Fetishes and psychiatry abound in this scathing comedy about a man and his father's argyle socks. *"John Patrick Shanley's new play, PSYCHOPATHIA SEXUALIS is ... perfectly poised between daffy comedy and believable human neurosis which Shanley combines so well ... "* –The LA Times. *"John Patrick Shanley's PSYCHOPATHIA SEXUALIS is a salty boulevard comedy with a bittersweet theme ... "* –New York Magazine. *"A tour de force of witty, barbed dialogue."* –Variety. [3M, 2W] ISBN: 0-8222-1615-9

DRAMATISTS PLAY SERVICE, INC.
440 Park Avenue South, New York, NY 10016 212-683-8960 Fax 212-213-1539
postmaster@dramatists.com www.dramatists.com

NEW PLAYS

• **A QUESTION OF MERCY by David Rabe.** The Obie Award-winning playwright probes the sensitive and controversial issue of doctor-assisted suicide in the age of AIDS in this poignant drama. *"There are many devastating ironies in Mr. Rabe's beautifully considered, piercingly clear-eyed work ... " –The NY Times. "With unsettling candor and disturbing insight, the play arouses pity and understanding of a troubling subject ... Rabe's provocative tale is an affirmation of dignity that rings clear and true."* –Variety. [6M, 1W] ISBN: 0-8222-1643-4

• **A DOLL'S HOUSE by Henrik Ibsen, adapted by Frank McGuinness. Winner of the 1997 Tony Award for best revival.** *"New, raw, gut-twisting and gripping. Easily the hottest drama this season."* –USA Today. *"Bold, brilliant and alive."* –The Wall Street Journal. *"A thunderclap of an evening that takes your breath away."* –Time. *"The stuff of Broadway legend."* –Associated Press. [4M, 4W, 2 boys] ISBN: 0-8222-1636-1

• **THE WAITING ROOM by Lisa Loomer.** Three women from different centuries meet in a doctor's waiting room in this dark comedy about the timeless quest for beauty -- and its cost. *" ... THE WAITING ROOM ... is a bold, risky melange of conflicting elements that is ... terrifically moving ... There's no resisting the fierce emotional pull of the play."* – The NY Times. *" ... one of the high points of this year's Off-Broadway season ... THE WAITING ROOM is well worth a visit."* –Back Stage. [7M, 4W, flexible casting] ISBN: 0-8222-1594-2

• **MR. PETERS' CONNECTIONS by Arthur Miller.** Mr. Miller describes the protagonist as existing in a dream-like state when the mind is "freed to roam from real memories to conjectures, from trivialities to tragic insights, from terror of death to glorying in one's being alive." With this memory play, the Tony Award and Pulitzer Prize-winner reaffirms his stature as the world's foremost dramatist. *" ... a cross between Joycean stream-of-consciousness and Strindberg's dream plays, sweetened with a dose of William Saroyan's philosophical whimsy ... CONNECTIONS is most intriguing ... Miller scholars will surely find many connections of their own to make between this work and the author's earlier plays."* –The NY Times. [5M, 3W] ISBN: 0-8222-1687-6

• **THE STEWARD OF CHRISTENDOM by Sebastian Barry.** A freely imagined portrait of the author's great-grandfather, the last Chief Superintendent of the Dublin Metropolitan Police. *"MAGNIFICENT ... the cool, elegiac eye of James Joyce's THE DEAD; the bleak absurdity of Samuel Beckett's lost, primal characters; the cosmic anger of KING LEAR ... "* –The NY Times. *"Sebastian Barry's compassionate imaging of an ancestor he never knew is among the most poignant onstage displays of humanity in recent memory."* –Variety. [5M, 4W] ISBN: 0-8222-1609-4

• **SYMPATHETIC MAGIC by Lanford Wilson. Winner of the 1997 Obie for best play.** The mysteries of the universe, and of human and artistic creation, are explored in this award-winning play. *"Lanford Wilson's idiosyncratic SYMPATHETIC MAGIC is his BEST PLAY YET ... the rare play you WANT ... chock-full of ideas, incidents, witty or poetic lines, scientific and philosophical argument ... you'll find your intellectual faculties racing."* – New York Magazine. *"The script is like a fully notated score, next to which most new plays are cursory lead sheets."* –The Village Voice. [5M, 3W] ISBN: 0-8222-1630-2

DRAMATISTS PLAY SERVICE, INC.
440 Park Avenue South, New York, NY 10016 212-683-8960 Fax 212-213-1539
postmaster@dramatists.com www.dramatists.com